Domestic VIOLENCE

WHAT EVERY PASTOR NEEDS TO KNOW

REVEREND AL MILES

FORTRESS PRESS

DOMESTIC VIOLENCE
What Every Pastor Needs to Know

Cover design by Nicole Sletten
Author photo by Kathy Miles
Book design by Michelle L. Norstad

Library of Congress Cataloging-in-Publication Data
Miles, Al, 1951–
    Domestic violence : what every pastor needs to know / Al Miles.
        p. cm.
    Includes bibliographical references.
    ISBN 0-8006-3175-7 (alk. paper)
    1. Church work with problem families. 2. Family violence—Religious aspects—Christianity. I. Title.
BV4438.5 .M54 2000
261.8'327—dc21   99-051589

The paper used in this publication meets the minimum requirements of American National Standard for Information Sciences—Permanence of Paper for Printed Library Materials, ANSI Z329.48-1984. ⊛ ™

Manufactured in the U.S.A.   AF 1-3175
12   11   10   09   8   9   10

Contents

This book is dedicated to my wife, Kathy, who is helping me with a lifelong struggle to shed the many unhealthy messages about control, power, and violence piled on American males. I also dedicate the book to William A. Smith, professor emeritus of Luther Seminary and my spiritual director. Bill is teaching me to take care of my own body, mind, and soul as I care for others.

The monotony of a church board meeting was broken by a woman's screams and the sounds of a frantic scuffle in the next room. To their horror, the board discovered a highly respected church member being strangled by her husband on top of a ping-pong table. Several of the men dragged the husband into the pastor's study for prayer and counseling. As the pastor was later to explain to me, he was untrained for such an emergency, but he did his best. After prayer, the repentant husband promised that he would never again behave in such a way, and so he was sent home to a reconciliation with his wife. By morning he phoned the pastor to say that he had killed his wife. Fortunately, the paramedics were able to resuscitate her in the ambulance on the way to the hospital. The woman had been deeply involved in the ministry of the church and a leader in its Christian school. The congregation became bitterly divided over what course of action they should expect, indeed demand, of *her*. Should the priority be to save a life even at the possible expense of the marriage or to save the marriage even at the possible expense of a human life? Neither pastor nor congregation was prepared for the crisis, and the result was a church split.

Like most clergy, the pastor had few resources with which to approach a dismayingly prevalent problem, nor could he give constructive guidance to his flock on this issue. Domestic violence ranks as the number one public health problem for women in America, and yet those of the cloth prefer to look the other way. They know, of course, that incidents do happen, but not in *their* congregation. Their folk are too nice, too spiritual, too well taught, too well balanced, too mature, too upstanding, and too discreet. A prime defense is to deny that the problem exists, even though the evidence tells us that there is a strong likelihood of spousal abuse in every faith community. If an admission must be made, pastors often minimize, conceal, or ignore the reality. Few dare to speak directly to the perpetrator about the problem. Many prefer to dodge so embarrassing and uncomfortable an issue. The truth is that they simply do not know what to do in abusive family situations. Many clergypersons have followed popular evangelical trends in idolizing and idealizing the family. The Bible, however, speaks forthrightly of troubled families and of God's redemptive work among them. Honesty, not silence, is the key to healing.

Often the pastor's theological framework simply does not permit an honest appraisal of the situation. They hold that marriage is a picture of Christ's love for the church, though Scripture indicates rather that Christ's love for the church is a paradigm for earthly marriage. Abuse, whether physical, sexual, verbal, or emotional, cannot possibly depict God's attitudes or actions. The pastor who would truly give pastoral care must first wrestle with theological issues such as those of headship and submission, hierarchy within the family, the relationship between man and woman, forgiveness, and the responsibility of a faith community toward victim, perpetrator, and children. Few are equipped to give either counseling or practical help in times of crisis. Many are reluctant to use the resources available within the community, even when the need for safety is crucial. Seldom have our seminaries given adequate training in this field, either in the philosophical or practical realm. Although victims turn more often to their pastors than to all other resources combined, clergy and other pastoral ministers simply have not been equipped to meet the challenge.

It is precisely here that this work of Aldean Miles is invaluable. His experience in years of working as a hospital chaplain has shown him the devastation wreaked in Christian families and the inadequacy of clergy when they are most needed. Thus it was that he began to hold seminars for Christian leaders to convince them of the reality of the problem, to lay out a theological framework that would enable them to obey the biblical mandate to rescue the victim from the hand of the violent, and to bring God's healing to all members of the family. His extensive interviews of survivors from various traditions demonstrate the impact of abuse on their spirituality. Too often we have been deaf to their hurt, but Al Miles gives these victims a voice. He also gives us the words of actual pastors and thereby affords us some astonishing insights. Because of the great diversity within Christian churches, Rev. Miles addresses persons of varying theological stripes and convictions. He offers sound biblical precepts and insights. The overall work is a prophetic one.

It is the task of the prophet to view the sin of a society, to make it a matter of prayer and contemplation, to bring the word of God to bear upon it, and to propose appropriate action. In this counsel to pastors, Al Miles has served as true prophet, obeying the scriptural command to "equip the saints for ministry" (Ephesians 4:12). This book calls those who are faithful to the word of God to do the work of God.

—CATHERINE CLARK KROEGER, PRESIDENT EMERITA, CHRISTIANS FOR BIBLICAL EQUALITY AND ADJUNCT ASSOCIATE PROFESSOR OF CLASSICAL AND MINISTRY STUDIES, GORDON-CONWELL THEOLOGICAL SEMINARY

Acknowledgments

Many people graciously gave time and wisdom that supported me throughout the research and writing of this book. I thank Jesus Christ for all of these individuals. I also thank Jesus Christ for his empowerment, guidance, and love, which kept me focused and inspired even during the times when I felt discouraged and frustrated.

I cannot overemphasize the contributions of my wife, Kathy. She stabilized me through every trial and triumph. I especially appreciate Kathy's patience and understanding, particularly on those weekends I spent researching and writing this book. Kathy read every draft of my handwritten notes, typed and retyped the manuscript, and both affirmed and challenged my arguments.

Appreciation must also be extended to Henry French and the staff of Augsburg Fortress Publishers for giving me the opportunity to have my work published with such a fine organization. Their editorial suggestions made my points much stronger. The same gratitude must be offered to Victoria A. Rebeck, my personal editor. Her skills helped to clarify and enliven my thoughts.

A host of other people were invaluable throughout the project. They read the manuscript, made insightful comments, suggested people to interview, and assisted in many other scholarly and technical ways. I extend a warm *mahalo* to George Apter, Barbara Chandler, Jeffery Chandler, Nelda Rhoades Clarke, Janice Brazil-Cummings, Diana Davids, Laura Delaplain, Curtiss Paul DeYoung, Fritz Fritschel, Antoinette Gray, Dolly Grimes-Johnson, L. Kevin Hamberger, Anne Marie Hunter, the people of Interfaith Network Against Domestic Violence, Joan Ishibashi, Jason Kimura, Catherine Clark Kroeger, Lydia Mae Koh Bolosan Kumasaka, the staff of Logos Productions, Inc., Julie Mall, James Earl Massey, Craig Mayfield, Melody Moody, Suzan Morrissette, Julie A. Owens, Molly Pandorf, Peggy Sanderford, William A. Smith, the staff of Sojourner Truth House, Cary Speaker, Carolyn Staats, Kathy Stresman, Lenore E. Walker, Connie Wiletzky, and Yvonne Yim.

Last, I have special appreciation for the fifty-two survivors of domestic violence who tell their stories in this book. Although most of these women's names were changed and certain aspects of their stories altered to ensure their anonymity and safety, the survivors eagerly participated. They expressed the hope that their stories would help make clergy and other pastoral ministers more sensitive to the emotional and spiritual needs of all victims. I thank these women for their courage and trust.

Preface. Clergy Voices

"Domestic abuse is one of the last dirty little secrets of our society. Too often, members of the clergy are guilty of assisting in the coverup, either by failing to notice the signs of abuse or by believing that it is best not to address the problem publicly. We clergy must better inform ourselves of the scope of this tragedy, recognize our own limitations, and begin to use the resources available to us. Al Miles's book is an important first step in that direction."

—REV. PATRICK HANDLSON, PRESBYTERIAN MINISTER AND PASTOR OF FIRST PRESBYTERIAN CHURCH (U.S.A.), HASTINGS, MINNESOTA

"Because domestic violence devastates so many families, clergy need to be on the front line of awareness and understanding of this concern. As we learn more about the dynamics and complexities of domestic violence, we are increasingly more able to provide life-affirming pastoral care to suffering families in our congregations. Al Miles brings to his writing a wealth of pastoral experience with victims and perpetrators, as well as a background in clergy consultation around domestic violence awareness. His valuable work speaks to pastors across a range of theological perspectives, from evangelicals to conservatives to liberals."

—REV. DR. LAURA DELAPLAIN, MINISTER IN THE UNITED METHODIST CHURCH AND DIRECTOR OF THE NORMA KENT PASTORAL COUNSELING CENTER, ABINGTON, MASSACHUSETTS

"One of the most critical issues of theology today is power. It informs our views of God and affects our relationships. Inappropriate and misleading images of divine power have contributed, I believe, to the unfortunate misuse of power in human relations. The church, both

11

clergy and laity, can benefit from learning about domestic violence, especially the role of power in the phenomenon. Power that respects and encourages freedom and full participation of people can be admirable and worth promoting. In this book Al Miles addresses all of these issues."

—Rev. Fritz Fritschel, Minister in the Evangelical Lutheran Church in America and Assisting Pastor of the Lutheran Church of Honolulu, Honolulu, Hawaii

"It is not every day that we clergy can read material that reaches our hearts, souls, and minds while requiring us to reflect on our lives and those of people who look to us for spiritual comfort and guidance. This book does just that. Those who read Al Miles's book will be moved to search the Scriptures and to seek additional information and training on domestic violence, a sensitive and dark area of reality. This book helps us to get beyond the cloak that hides domestic violence and moves us to Christian social action. This journey might be the greatest challenge some clergy have ever faced."

—Rev. Janice Brazil-Cummings, Minister in the African Methodist Episcopal Church and Regional Director for the State of Wisconsin Department of Corrections, Division of Community Corrections, Milwaukee, Wisconsin

"Al Miles's book is a must-read for all clergy, male and female. Miles's work comes to us in a time when an estimated one in four women will suffer some sort of abuse in their lifetimes. I have found this statistic no less true of the women in the churches I have served, yet nothing in seminary taught me how to provide pastoral care to victims and abusers. Many clergy I have talked to also lacked such training. This void has caused some of us to ignore the problem and others of us to advise people to do nothing else than to pray. Al Miles has filled that void with solid information, challenges, and suggestions. His work gives clergy the information they need to speak a prophetic voice against violence in what ought to be loving *relationships. He also challenges us to be answers to the prayers of victims and their families."*

—REV. E. DANIEL SMITH, EPISCOPAL PRIEST AND PASTOR OF ST. TIMOTHY'S EPISCOPAL CHURCH, WEST DES MOINES, IOWA

"At our best we clergy think we are sensitive to the issue of domestic violence because we are sympathetic to victims. At our worst we ourselves are perpetrators of violence through our preaching and our behavior. Al Miles has written a book that clearly shows how much work we need to do in the church to address the issue of domestic violence. He leads us on an often painful journey, sharing stories of horror and healing, teaching us how we can truly minister in these broken situations and bring a message of justice and hope."

—REV. JOAN ISHIBASHI, MINISTER IN THE UNITED CHURCH OF CHRIST AND ASSOCIATE CONFERENCE MINISTER FOR ADMINISTRATION AND RESOURCES, HONOLULU, HAWAII

"Al Miles's book is for pastors and lay leaders in every congregation. Many of the hurts people experience are silent hurts. How do we speak to the hurt so real and yet voiceless? How do we let victims know that we care and that we understand? This book helps us to rethink one of our most valuable ministries—reaching out to the hurting. There are more victims of domestic violence in our churches than most of us imagine. This book will help you as you struggle with this difficult issue."

—REV. DR. ROGER LOVETTE, SOUTHERN BAPTIST MINISTER AND PASTOR OF THE BAPTIST CHURCH OF THE COVENANT, BIRMINGHAM, ALABAMA

"Domestic violence is an issue that women face throughout life. Every pastor needs to condemn the abuse of women and children, regardless of the form it takes. We need to help our parishioners to accept victims and to help them address their pain. Rev. Miles's book

is an essential resource for those churches that will deal with domestic violence in a loving and supportive way."

—Rev. Nelda Rhoades Clarke, Minister in the Church of the Brethren and Executive Director of the Emma Norton Residence, St. Paul, Minnesota

"Domestic violence is a complex problem in today's society. This complexity is manifested in the physical, emotional, verbal, and sexual dimensions of the phenomena itself. Therefore, it is critical that ordained ministers acknowledge this issue as well and learn about its potential and direction. It is fundamental to serve people in the spirit of the Gospel. The ordained minister must also be an agent of healing for victims and an agent of reconciliation for perpetrators. This will contribute to the transformation of our world in the kingdom that we are all called to live in and celebrate. Al Miles's book is both timely and noteworthy. It behooves clergy and laity alike to take advantage of his insight and wisdom regarding this subject. It is a work that must not be missed."

—Rev. Michael McDermott, Catholic Priest and Pastor of Saints Peter and Paul Church, St. Paul, Nebraska

Introduction.
"Where Are All the Pastors?"

Where are all the pastors? This question became a refrain throughout my hour-long keynote address in Milwaukee on that rainy Friday morning, May 2, 1997. I'd traveled to the city from Honolulu to take part in an all-day conference, "Working Toward Family Peace— A Walk Together," on domestic and family violence. The brainchild of Sojourner Truth House, a local organization dedicated to the prevention and elimination of violence in families, the conference sought to bring together individuals from a wide variety of cultures, races, and professions to dialogue about the ongoing pervasive problem of violence in the home. One of the groups the conference organizers had hoped would attend in great numbers, I learned, were parish pastors.

Kathy Stresman, at the time the community education coordinator for Sojourner Truth House and my main contact throughout the nearly two years of planning for this event, informed me that 1,200 conference brochures had been mailed to pastors in and around Milwaukee. In addition, Kathy said, many of these same spiritual leaders had received a personal invitation from either her or one of the other Sojourner Truth House staff or board members.

The thought of having significant clergy attendance at the conference made me feel even more excited and honored to have been asked to participate. Since the early 1990s, when I began publishing articles and speaking about the important role pastors can play in the prevention and eradication of domestic and family violence—especially among the people worshiping within our congregations—I had noticed that clergy members on the whole, and especially male clergy, were conspicuously absent when these subjects were being addressed. The lack of pastoral involvement was also observed by the individuals who consistently attended the workshops at which I spoke: lay Christian women, victims and non-victims alike. By the mid 1990s, the general consensus these women expressed was the belief that most clergy members simply did not care for their well-being.

Embarrassed and often feeling defensive, I, too, was having a difficult time explaining or understanding the lack of pastoral involvement. Several times each year the hospital at which I was then the director of chaplaincy would host pastoral care conferences on a number of moral issues. The workshops least attended, by far, were the ones dealing with the problem of violence in the home. Further, even though many pastors invited me to speak at their churches on this subject, seldom would any of them attend the sessions. This was especially true of male pastors.

Angered and frustrated by this lack of pastoral participation, I developed a policy: I'd speak on domestic or family violence issues only at those churches where the pastors themselves agreed to attend the workshops. I soon discovered that this course of action was also not foolproof. Many clergy members readily agreed to my stated condition of being present at the workshops. But, shortly after the sessions started, the pastors would mysteriously disappear and never return. When I began confronting clergypeople about this behavior, they all offered the same justification: an unexpected emergency had arisen, I was told. Curiously, these "emergencies" rarely occurred when I spoke on other topics.

The past weighed heavily on my mind as I stood in front of the 135 well-dressed women and men in Milwaukee moments before beginning my keynote address on that spring day in 1997. The Sojourner Truth House staff had done an excellent job of promoting the conference. Arriving an hour before my talk, I met men and women from a variety of cultural and racial backgrounds. These individuals were serving the greater Milwaukee metropolitan area in professions such as education, health care, psychology, and social work, as well as serving in other justice and social service programs throughout the community.

I did not meet any parish pastors during that hour and this concerned me. Were they running late? Had they gotten stuck in traffic?

I was still hopeful of a large clergy turnout. As I walked to the podium on the stage of that lovely auditorium moments after being introduced by Kathy Stresman, I thought about what she had told me months earlier: 1,200 brochures were mailed out to area pastors, and several of these clergypeople had also received a personal invitation. How many spiritual leaders were actually in attendance? I decided to solve this mystery right away by asking all of the pastors in the audience to please stand.

Less than ten people stood up.

Where are all the pastors? I asked with contempt. The few clergy in attendance did not seem to know. "I just assumed that the room would be full of clergy folks," responded one male pastor. "Maybe they all had other commitments," surmised another male clergy, defensively. But many of the individuals working in other professional disciplines said that the poor pastoral turnout was status quo. "It's been the same story wherever I've lived," lamented a woman working as a child and family advocate. "Few pastors ever attend conferences on domestic or family violence. Tell me, how in the world do they expect to help abused women and children without proper education and training?"

Throughout the day in the two workshops I conducted, during small group discussions and in one-to-one conversations, many of the conferees expressed frustration and outrage at the ongoing lack of involvement by clergy members in the care of abused women and children. The feedback was similar to the groundswell of disgust I was beginning to receive at other conferences, both throughout the Mainland and in my home state of Hawaii. Wherever I traveled to speak on domestic and family violence issues, professionals and victims alike were asking one primary question: Where are all the pastors?

Although this was not the first, or the last, symposium at which clergy were poorly represented when the topic focused on violence against women and children, the conference in Milwaukee compelled me to write this book. The magnitude of pastoral neglect— less than ten clergy members in attendance when 1,200 brochures had been sent to ordained ministers—jolted me out of my own state of denial into reality. No longer could I think that pastors weren't coming to seminars on violence against women and children because they had scheduling conflicts or emergencies to tend to, the two most common excuses clergy had been giving me. I was forced to face the fact that many clergypeople were willfully choosing to avoid these issues.

But why? Why would spiritual leaders intentionally neglect abused women and children? Do we think there are no abused women worshiping in our congregations? Why aren't clergypeople willing to seek the education and training that could help save women and children a lot of suffering, even death? I didn't know it at the time, but soon I'd be searching for answers to these troubling questions. "Somebody has to do something to help clergy members understand that our lack of involvement with abused women and children is making matters much worse for these victims," I reported angrily to my wife when I phoned her back home shortly after the conference in Milwaukee had concluded. "If somebody doesn't do something and fast," I raged, "then battered women and children will have to continue to live without the spiritual care they need and deserve."

That night I could not sleep. My mind was a sea of turbulence. Somebody had to talk to clergypeople to find out what's preventing most of us from becoming involved in domestic and family violence issues. Somebody. In the middle of that long night, I arose from my tossing and turning and began jotting down sentence fragments on hotel stationery.

Domestic and family violence . . . too broad together . . . Choose one or the other . . . Talk with tons of clergy, variety of denominations. Interview lots of victims, all of them Christians. Talk with former batterers who've worked on issues for years . . . Speak to wide range of experts.

Questions began popping into my head that "somebody" would need to ask clergy. For some reason, all of these questions focused on domestic rather than family abuse. Do you believe domestic violence is wrong? Are there domestic violence victims and perpetrators worshiping in your congregation? How are you caring for victims and dealing with perpetrators? Can you name and describe the various forms of abuse? Have you ever heard of the cycle of violence? Can you describe the various aspects of this cycle? What education and training opportunities on domestic violence have you taken advantage of in your community? Are you working in collaboration with professionals from other fields to ensure the overall safety and well-being of battered women and their dependent children?

I still did not know that the "somebody" needing to work on this project was me. That realization came later in the morning when I was saying goodbye to Kathy Stresman and, spontaneously, I announced that I would be writing a book on domestic violence. Issues of *family violence,* which include but are not limited to child abuse, elder abuse, and animal abuse, also need careful study by clergy and other pastoral workers because these, too, have reached far beyond epidemic proportions. In this book, however, those issues will be addressed only as they relate to *domestic abuse:* that is, the violence perpetrated by a person against a current or former intimate partner. I recognize that there are also a small percentage of men who are violated by an intimate or former intimate partner. However, with more than two million American women being assaulted by their partners each year,[1] we will focus our attention here on abused and battered women.

The six chapters of this book are the result of my reading a number of books and articles and conducting interviews with 158 Catholic and Protestant clergy, 52 survivors, 46 professionals working in the domestic violence field in a number of specialized areas, and 21 former batterers.

The importance of talking with clergy from many different theological perspectives who could bring concerns from a variety of viewpoints was quickly revealed. There was a strong sense that many of the ordained ministers I interviewed were attempting to pigeon-hole me theologically. For example, before agreeing to be interviewed I had anticipated that some clergy would want to know my beliefs and thoughts about why men abuse women and, perhaps, my qualifications to write this book. But that was not the case. Only one of the 158 clergypeople, a woman, wanted to know my thoughts on why men abuse women. All the other clergy members focused their inquiries on doctrinal issues: What is your denominational background? What does your church teach about the authority of Scripture, divorce, and homosexuality? How long have you been born again? Curiously, not one of these clergypeople asked anything about my beliefs or thoughts on domestic violence.

One other issue needs to be addressed here. It concerns how to use the book. In my interviews of 158 ordained ministers, I encountered a great deal of denial, fear, and resistance to the idea that abused women and their perpetrators were members of the pastors' congregations. Therefore, those of us who have had the opportunity to be educated and trained in dealing with the myriad complexities associated with domestic violence, whether we are clergy members, survivors, or work in a variety of other disciplines within the movement, will need to act as resource people to reluctant spiritual leaders. Invite these clergypeople to classes, workshops, ministerial retreats, etc., and make the book the topic of discussion. Or give a copy of the book to a disinclined clergy member and tell them you look forward to discussing the material in a few weeks. Be sure you set a specific time to review the book, however. If you do not, it makes it too easy for a reluctant pastor to put the book aside and never read it.

Where are all the pastors? What will it take for us to commit ourselves to providing better care to abused women? How many more victims will have to suffer or die before we begin reading the articles and books, and purchasing the videotapes that can help educate us? When will all clergypeople realize that our absence at conferences, workshops, and training sessions on domestic violence is depriving victims of the effective and sensitive pastoral care that is essential to ensure the safety and well-being of battered women and their children? This book will begin to provide readers with answers to these very important questions.

Chapter 1. Encouraging and Excusing Men/Blaming Women

I think there's been a conspiracy of silence in the church regarding domestic violence. Most victims don't come to their pastors. They are ashamed, embarrassed, and fear that their pastors will condemn or reject them, or encourage them to stay in an abusive relationship, or that male pastors will side with the husband. Prior to my becoming involved, some thirty years into my pastoral career, I think maybe only two or three women who were victims of domestic violence had come to me.

— REV. ROBERT S. OWENS, JR., MINISTER IN THE PRESBYTERIAN CHURCH (U.S.A.) (RETIRED)

"Such a Great Guy"

"Get off the fucking phone, you goddamn bitch!" I heard a man shout angrily. His words became muffled as Rita placed her hands over the receiver, but I could still hear him yelling. Suddenly, the phone crashed against the floor and I heard Rita scream. It was an awful sound, as though she had been thrown into a vat of boiling water. Overwhelmed and terrified, I did not know how I could free Rita from the grasp of this unidentified assailant. My ear was glued to the receiver. I was afraid to listen further, yet more afraid of leaving Rita completely alone with this disturbed man.

Finally, in a voice filled with horror, Rita picked up the phone and hurriedly said, "Al, I've got to go!" The man called her a bitch again and then the receiver slammed down. I was totally unnerved. My mind was racing. I wondered if I should dial 911 and then quickly drive to Rita's home. My phone rang while I was still pondering. Rita was calling me back. Her intention was to assure me, and perhaps herself, that everything was all right.

She apologized for what she called "another of Walt's bad moods." He had now left their home to cool off. It sounded far more serious than a person experiencing a bad mood, I said. Walt's behavior was abusive and violent. I asked if he hit her. After hesitating for several moments, Rita denied ever being struck by Walt. Although I did not believe her, I decided not to push matters just then.

That night I could not sleep. My mind kept playing the scene of Walt's verbal and probable physical abuse of Rita and her scream of terror. I wondered if I should have called the police or, at the very least, asked Rita to spend the night with my wife and me. At four A.M. I was consumed with the fear that Walt might have killed his wife. Around 6:30 A.M. Rita made an unscheduled visit to my office. As she stood in the doorway, I tried desperately not to betray the overwhelming sense of fear and concern I had for her safety. Tears ran down her face as she slowly settled into a chair. Moments later she began disclosing the countless acts of violence that Walt had perpetrated against her over the course of their fifteen-year marriage—physical beatings using his fists, feet, and other objects during his "bad moods." In addition, Rita said Walt constantly called her such demeaning names as "bitch," "cunt," "slut," and "whore." On several occasions he had threatened to kill her.

I suggested to Rita that we go either to the office of a colleague of mine who specialized in supporting victims of domestic violence or to the director of a shelter for battered women. She quickly replied, "Oh, I'm not one of those women. I'll be all right. I just have to somehow learn to be a better wife."

In the more than eighteen years I have served as a hospital chaplain, hundreds of women have disclosed to me the episodes of violence inflicted upon them by their husbands or boyfriends. Like Rita, most of these victims (whom I will also refer to as "survivors") have either assumed the blame for their abuse, or have been faulted by their abusers or other people. And almost none of these victims has identified herself as a battered woman.

The abuse of women throughout the world—emotional, psychological, physical, sexual, spiritual, and verbal—has exceeded epidemic proportions. The violence is not the result of a victim's failure to be a good wife, girlfriend, mother, Christian, sex partner, or person. Instead, domestic abuse is usually perpetrated by men who desire to have power and control over their female intimate partners. Complicating matters are the many ways in which our society encourages and excuses male violence, and blames the victims. Glance at a newspaper or magazine, play a CD or tape, turn on a radio or television, go to a movie or rent a video, or surf the Internet and you'll be confronted by images of men brutalizing women. The abusers' defense is "She made me do it" or "She started it."

Clergypeople have often not been helpful in dealing with the problem of domestic violence. While many women affirm the overall value of their religious faith, few say that spiritual leaders have supported their struggle to leave an abusive situation. In fact, several women have told me that their pastors' responses have stifled their healing process. Clergy say things like, "You have to work harder at being a better wife"; "Submit yourself to your husband. He is the head of you, as Christ is the head of the church"; "Pray so that you'll be able to endure this pain. Remember, God will never give you more than you can bear"; "Divorce is a sin. You must do everything possible to keep your family together"; and "The wife does not rule over her own body, but the husband does"—the same phrases perpetrators often use.

Let's return to Rita and Walt. Two days after telling me about Walt's abuse, Rita stopped by my office again. She said she might feel comfortable discussing her situation with her minister, Pastor Carl. He had known Rita since birth and had officiated at her baptism, confirmation, and wedding. I also knew Pastor Carl. He attended many of the conferences I hosted for clergy, religious workers, and health care professionals at the children's hospital at which I was director of pastoral care at the time. (A teacher at a Christian elementary school, Rita often attended these programs as well.) Carl always told me he appreciated the sessions on child abuse, comforting parents who experience the death of an infant, and the ethical and moral issues arising out of caring for premature babies. Ironically, just a month before I heard over the telephone Walt abuse his wife, Rita and Pastor Carl attended my hospital's conference "Violence in the Home: How Clergy Can Help Survivors."

During that symposium I gave an hour plenary talk on the abuse I had experienced while growing up. At the conclusion of my session, Pastor Carl was the first person to greet me. He said very little other than to thank me for my courage and give me a big hug. This warm response to my pain made me feel good about Rita's decision to disclose her abuse with Pastor Carl. I thought he would provide excellent support to her, and that he would also confront Walt about his violent behavior.

I was wrong on both counts.

After meeting with her pastor, Rita immediately called my office. Her description of the session shocked me. "I told Pastor Carl all about Walt's violence," she began, her words nearly suffocated by tears. "He stared at me for a long time then finally replied, 'I just can't believe it. I've known Walt since he was a little kid. He wouldn't harm a flea. Why have you waited all these years to tell this story? Are you sure you're not exaggerating things? You could ruin your marriage and Walt's fine practice. [Walt was a prominent surgeon in the community.] He's such a great guy.'" Rita said she felt raped by her minister's words.

Rita gave me permission to speak with Pastor Carl. I met with him at his church office that same afternoon. He was neither apologetic nor defensive. "Al, I've known both Walt and Rita since they were babies," he explained. "They've been in love since their teens. I understand you unfortunately overheard a private spat between a husband and wife. Hell, married life is tough; every couple has arguments. Now Rita wants to throw everything away because she's a little upset."

I sat in disbelief. This could not have been the same man who only a month earlier had shown warm support to me when I disclosed the abuse in my history. I told Carl I was enraged by his attitude and also because he appeared to be blaming the victim, Rita, for Walt's violent behavior. This was not a quarrel between lovers, I said; Walt needed professional help or he would continue to victimize Rita and might even kill her.

I encouraged Carl to learn the facts about domestic violence and the dynamics associated with both survivors and batterers. I warned him that Rita was certainly not the only victim in his congregation of one thousand worshipers, and I was concerned that his lack of knowledge on the subject could put many other survivors in his parish at even greater risk. Carl disputed my assertion about other victims in the church. "In thirty-eight years of serving this congregation," he claimed, "not one woman has ever complained to me about being beaten by her husband." Nevertheless, he did agree to have me lead a month-long lecture series at his church on domestic violence.

More than one hundred people attended each session. Afterward, thirty-three women called or visited my office and disclosed the abuse they had experienced at the hands of their husbands or boyfriends. Many women were moved to seek help from professionals trained in the field. Rita attended every session and eventually joined a support group for survivors of domestic violence. She divorced Walt and now lives in another part of the country, where she pursues her commitment to help other abused women. (As I expected, Walt did not attend one session at the church.)

Neither did Pastor Carl.

The minister also never came to another of the conferences I led at the hospital. He would not even respond to any of the invitations I mailed him. At a chance meeting a few years later Carl said to me, "I know you've heard about Walt's and Rita's divorce. It's such a shame. Too bad they couldn't work out their differences. I still think Rita overreacted. Even if the abuse did happen, which I doubt, I know Walt's really sorry. He's such a great guy."

Biblical Sanctions or Scriptural Misinterpretations?

Our theology is shaped as much by the passages of Scripture we choose to ignore, as those we choose to cite.
—Rev. John Tschudy, United Church of Christ Minister, Pastor of St. John's United Church of Christ, Slinger, Wisconsin

On Saturday, February 11, 1995, an article I wrote about men's violence appeared in the religion section of *The Honolulu Advertiser*.[1] I
challenged men to look closely at the many ways we perpetrate the
emotional, physical, psychological, sexual, spiritual, and verbal
abuse of women and children with our attitudes, actions, apathy, and
beliefs. I warned that if we did not acknowledge our abuse, repent,
seek professional help, and learn how to manage our anger, rage, and
power, and control needs, we would continue to destroy women,
children, and ourselves. Reactions to the article were swift and
strong. Female clergy, laity, and professionals from across the state
thanked me for my directness and honesty. Men from a variety of
cultural, ethnic, faith, and socioeconomic backgrounds described
the article as disturbing, but also said it was needed and truthful.
Ironically, though the piece was addressed to men and boys from all
ages and groups, male clergy reacted with the most hostility. They
branded me as a "ball-busting feminist," "heretic," "lesbian lover,"
"left winger," "male basher," and "troublemaker."

The harshest criticism came from the senior pastor serving one
of the largest churches in Hawaii. Calling me a "man-hating liberal
with obvious ties to the American Civil Liberties Union," the minister predicted the article would encourage more women to "go
astray," forsaking their proper God-given roles in church and home,
and to follow "a pack of lies." When I asked the minister to elaborate
on the lies I told in my article he replied, "Radical feminists like
yourself are deceiving and polluting righteous Christian women
across America with your lies about females being equal to males."
The pastor then introduced the Bible into what was becoming a sermon. "The Scriptures are crystal clear, Rev. Miles," he extolled in an
escalating voice. "Even in all your liberalism you must agree that
man is the ruler of woman, as Christ is the ruler of his church."
When I told the minister I strongly disagreed with his biblical interpretation of headship, explaining that the Scriptures espouse an
equal partnership between women and men rather than male dominance, he became unglued. "You must have received your theology
degree from one of those liberal-minded, gay-loving seminaries on
the West Coast," he coldly surmised. "I'm sure your professors

taught you that Jesus wasn't born of a virgin, and same-sex marriage is blessed by God." I knew any further discussion would be pointless.

That particular minister was unusually hostile. I am more troubled by clergy with far more balanced views who unwittingly encourage and excuse the violence men perpetrate against women, often using the Bible as justification for their pastoral positions. For example, 158 ministers I interviewed while researching this book condemned domestic violence as deplorable, disgusting, sinful, and wrong. Yet, several of these same pastors, women as well as men, said they believe the Bible teaches that a man should be the "head" of his wife. Further, many pastors stated that wives should "submit" to their husbands, never mentioning a husband's responsibility whatsoever to his wife. When asked about divorce as an option for battered women, nearly all the clergy said victims should do everything possible to keep the family together. Once again, the responsibility of the perpetrating husband was inexplicably never mentioned. I reminded the pastors that suggesting a survivor stay in her home under violent circumstances jeopardizes the safety of both the victim and her children. Given that warning, several clergy then said they would encourage victims to seek help from people working in shelters for battered women. Still, most of the ministers continued to view divorce as an option for the victim only after all other avenues of support and attempts to reconcile the relationship with her offending partner had been exhausted.

Finally, while nearly all of the pastors I interviewed said they frequently preach on family values, only a few said that they address the issue of domestic violence from the pulpit, classroom, during times of community prayer, or in any other setting. (I'll introduce several ministers throughout the book, especially in chapter 6, who do deal with the problem.) I interviewed clergymen and clergywomen serving in parishes, counseling centers, and institutions across the country. They identified themselves as conservative, evangelical, fundamental, liberal, mainline, moderate, and progressive.

Unfortunately, the responses I got mirror the extensive research conducted by Nancy Nason-Clark, a professor of sociology at the University of New Brunswick. She found that while 31 percent of clergy in Canada claim to have preached specific messages on wife and/or child abuse and 40 percent indicate they have discussed the problem of family violence in all of their premarital counseling, very few women parishioners can recall any such sermons. Further, Nason-Clark found that some clergy believe they are preaching against violence when their text is the stoning of Stephen or Jesus' condemnation of the Pharisees who brought the adulterous woman to him. When preachers do not directly condemn the abuse of women, survivors have understood their remarks as support for it.[2]

Do the Scriptures indicate that men are superior to women? Are husbands ordained by God to be the head of their wives? Should wives have to submit to their husbands? What is written about the ways in which husbands should treat their wives? Is the family unit so sacred that divorce is to be considered only after all other means of resolve have failed—even when a woman and her children are in grave danger? Let us look to the Scriptures as we consider these questions.

Male Headship/Female Submission

Male headship sets the stage for domestic violence. I don't subscribe to that in any way, shape, or form. When we talk about a man and a woman in the sacrament of matrimony, we're talking about a partnership, people working together. One partner is just as much the expression of God's creation as the other.

—FATHER MICHAEL MCDERMOTT, CATHOLIC PRIEST AND PASTOR OF SAINTS PETER AND PAUL CHURCH, ST. PAUL, NEBRASKA

Those who promote a hierarchical ordering of the sexes often cite Genesis 2 and 3 for support. Because the text is usually translated and interpreted as saying[3] that woman was created from man's rib (Gen. 2:18-25), the man named the woman (v. 23), the woman yielded to temptation and then offered the fruit to the man (3:1-7), and God "punished" the woman with these words: "Your desire will be for your husband, and he will rule over you" (3:16 NIV) proponents conclude that men are superior to women. They also use the work of fourth-century theologian Augustine to further strengthen their position. Augustine's interpretation of Genesis 2 and 3 is the basis of his doctrine of original sin, which, at its core, blames the woman for the introduction of sin and suffering into the world with temptation and sexuality. As Charles Ess writes in the book *Violence against Women and Children:* "Perhaps the single most important source in Western tradition for the image of Eve as (sexual) temptress and cause of sin is Augustine, the fourth-century theologian whose work powerfully shapes and defines Christian belief in both Roman Catholic and Protestant traditions. Augustine both develops the interpretation of the woman in Genesis 2–3 as the primary source of sin, and makes this interpretation a foundational element of what becomes the orthodox doctrine of Original Sin. In this way, Augustine embeds in Christian orthodoxy an image of the primordial woman which serves as a myth justifying the subordination of the female —especially as the female functions as a chaos agent who threatens male hierarchies."[4]

In addition, proponents of male headship/female submission point to the following New Testament texts to support their views: 1 Corinthians 11:2-16 and 14:34-35, Ephesians 5:21-33, and 1 Timothy 2:8-15. Some English translations (NIV and NRSV, for example) of these passages seem to further confirm to some readers that men are the "head" of women, just as Christ is the head of the church, and wives should "submit" to the "authority" of their husbands.

A more obscure text used to justify male headship is Isaiah 38:19, which in the NIV reads, "The living, the living—they praise you, as I am doing today; fathers tell their children about your faithfulness." I mention this text because it has been recited by a prominent spiritual leader, Promise Keepers' CEO, Bill McCartney.[5]

I have many problems with the male headship/female submission model in a marriage or other intimate partnership. First, it presents a dangerous structure. While power in and of itself does not damage (anymore than firearms on their own maim or kill), and certainly not everyone given authority abuses it, history has shown that power in the wrong hands has the great potential to hurt or destroy others. Recall the Nazi atrocities during World War II, apartheid in South Africa, "ethnic cleansing" in Bosnia and Kosovo, the continued problems associated with white racism in America, and the ill-treatment of women and girls by men and boys throughout the world. Giving undue power to individuals for the express purpose of their assuming authority over another person or group is, at the very least, dangerous.

When we tell men they are the authorities, heads, leaders, lords, masters, or rulers over their adult women partners, we are only a small step away from giving these men, especially those who are insecure, immature, or emotionally or psychologically unstable, permission to abuse women. When a pastor or spiritual leader reinforces the notion that men's authority over women is from God or Christ, men feel all the more justified in abusing women. Psychotherapist Carolyn Holderread Heggen writes: "We live in a violence-prone culture that particularly disrespects and despises the feminine. When such cultural inclinations are reinforced by religious teachings, they become even more influential and dangerous for women. No other human institution has more power to define and control relationships between women and men than organized religion. Particularly, nothing else has the power of organized religion to define 'woman's place' and to punish those women who step outside this religiously assigned role and violate the rules of patriarchy."[6]

Heggen's words illuminate a second problem with the male headship/female submission model—it robs women of their God-given power and blames them for the emotional, physical, psychological, sexual, spiritual, and verbal abuse they receive from their husbands or boyfriends. Patricia Riddle Gaddis, a shelter director for a domestic violence program, highlights an all too familiar paradox faced by victims. "While numerous members of the faith community advise the battered woman to 'submit' and 'pray harder for change within the marital relationship,' they also tend to blame the battered woman when she returns to her abusive spouse. One minister of a mainline denomination who has been known to advise battered women to 'submit and pray for a miracle' recently told me that he could not understand why battered women 'go back for more.' A paradoxical blaming pattern among many within the faith community holds the woman responsible for the violence yet harshly judges her for going back to her partner after an escape!"[7]

The male headship/female submission model makes it more difficult for vulnerable women to protect themselves or their children. As one survivor told me, "Since both my abusive husband and our pastor said the Bible demanded that I obey my husband even though he constantly beat me and raped our two little girls, I stayed in the home long after I realized his behavior was evil. However, for years I believed the abuse was caused by my not submitting fully to my husband's authority."

Heggen comments on these common feelings: "A female who believes she is morally defective and thus unable to trust her inner sense of what is right and wrong, who believes men reflect more of the divine image than women, and who believes it is her Christian duty to obey men may find it hard to confront an abusive man, particularly if he tells her, 'You're overreacting,' or, 'It's all in your head,' or, 'Trust me—there's nothing wrong.' When females don't trust themselves, they more easily give up their power and lose ability to confront and resist destructive things done to them or their children."[8]

The third reason I oppose the male headship/female submission model is that it not only destroys the esteem and personhood of women and demonstrates a destructive pattern that future generations may emulate, but it also keeps men from benefitting from a healthy intimate partnership. As we will see in chapter 4, former batterers who come to acknowledge their violence feel guilt and shame, as well as grief over the loss of a wife or girlfriend, children, jobs, and other family members and friends. Clergy members who teach the male headship/female submission model must shoulder some of the blame for the destruction it causes.

> *This time he accused me of flirting with our neighbor across the street. He had seen me talking to him the previous day and had decided that I was having an affair. I cringed as he began to quote Scriptures because I knew the beatings were always worse when he recited Bible verses. I think he felt absolved when he used the Bible. The beating must have gone on for over an hour, and in the process he punctured my eardrum and broke my wrist, not to mention all of the welts and bruises that covered my body.*[9]

Pastors and other spiritual leaders: Take heed as you instruct men to rule and women to submit. It is a dangerous paradigm that helps to encourage and excuse men's violence and then blames women for their own victimization.

Equality between Intimate Partners

We are called to equality, mutuality, and partnership. Thinking anything differently is outdated, misguided, vilifying, and potentially dangerous.

—Rev. Julie Mall, Minister, Presbyterian Church (U.S.A.), Minneapolis, Minnesota

The Book of Genesis

Revisiting the Hebrew and Christian Scriptures, looking at some of the same passages used by proponents of the male headship/female submission model and some other verses, we find that the Bible actually teaches equality between intimate partners (Another Creation Story: Genesis 1:26-28).

While proponents of the hierarchical view of the sexes usually cite only Genesis 2:18-25, which depicts woman's creation from man's rib, they don't mention a parallel account of the creation of woman and man in Genesis 1:26-27: "Then God said, 'Let us make humankind in our image, according to our likeness; and let them have dominion over the fish of the sea, and over the birds of the air, and over the cattle, and over all the wild animals of the earth, and over every creeping thing that creeps upon the earth.' So God created humankind in his image, in the image of God he created them; male and female he created them" (NRSV).

In his exegetical work on Genesis in *The New Interpreter's Bible*, Terence E. Fretheim writes, "That both male and female *are* so created (see also 5:2) means that the female images the divine as much as the male; both are addressed in the command of v. 28. The reference to both implies that their roles in life are not identical, and that likeness to God pertains not only to what they have in common but also to what remains distinctive about them (the emergence of both male and female images of God could be grounded in this text). The fact that the words *male* and *female* are not used for animals indicates that both sexuality and procreation are involved."[10]

In the second account of the creation of woman (Gen. 2:18-25), one should not infer male superiority/female inferiority. Fretheim states: "For the woman to be called 'helper' *(ēzer)*—a word used by both God and the narrator—carries no implications regarding the status of the one who helps; indeed, God is often called the helper of human beings (Psalm 121:1-2). The NRSV's 'partner' may capture the note of correspondence more than 'suitable' or 'fitting.' The notion of Eve as 'helper' cannot be collapsed into procreation, not least because the immediate outcome specified in verses 24-25 does not focus on this concern; the term does not offer evidence of a hierarchy."[11]

Although some proponents of the male headship/female submission model have understood woman's being created from man in Genesis 2:21-23 as an indication of male superiority, the Hebrew text does not bear this out. "The relationship of the woman to the 'rib' entails no subordination, any more than man's being created from the ground implies his subordination to it. . . . Unlike the dust, the rib is living material. The theological force of this creation is implied in 1:26-27—namely, the explicit equality of man and woman in the image of God (being created first or last remains immaterial). The description of the human creation emphasizes the personal attention implicit in the image of God as builder."[12]

We read in Genesis 2:23 that after woman is created, "the man said, 'This is now bone of my bones and flesh of my flesh; she shall be called woman, for she was taken out of man'" (NIV). Proponents of male dominance claim man's naming of woman as support for their view. But once again, the text carries no such indication. "For the woman to be named by the man does not subordinate the named to the namer, any more than does Hagar's naming of God subordinate the deity to her (16:13)."[13]

Let us now revisit the temptation of humankind as told in Genesis 3:1-7. For centuries, men—including pastors and other spiritual leaders—have read these verses with spiritual blinders on.

I grew up being told by my pastor and still hear male clergy today describing Eve as a naive, gullible woman who, after falling to temptation, seduced poor innocent Adam to do the same. This interpretation is simply another example of men blaming women for actions we have either initiated or in which we readily participated. In fact, this starts in Genesis 3:12, where part of the man's sin is his blaming the woman for his decision to partake of the fruit! Fretheim observes, "The woman takes some of the fruit and gives it to her husband. As a silent partner 'with her' [many translations omit "with her"] throughout this exchange, the man puts up no resistance, raises no questions, and considers no theological issues; he simply and silently takes his turn. The woman does not act as a temptress in this scene; they both have succumbed to the same source of temptation. They stand together as 'one flesh' at this point as well."[14]

The New Testament

> We've learned to use scriptures as a club. Women have heard it again and again that they're supposed to submit to male authority. This, of course, is much bigger than what the scriptures actually say, but it's been taught nonetheless. Scriptures have often been taken out of context—and we continue to pass on these skewed teachings.
>
> —REVEREND NELDA RHOADES CLARKE, MINISTER IN THE
> CHURCH OF THE BRETHREN AND EXECUTIVE DIRECTOR OF THE
> EMMA NORTON RESIDENCE, ST. PAUL, MINNESOTA

The New Testament has been a source of forgiveness, freedom, hope, love, and reconciliation for millions of Christians and those of other faiths. Many victims of domestic violence, however, have felt oppressed and denounced by some interpretations of New Testament texts. Many pastors have played a major role in this problem. I have heard horrific stories of battered women disclosing their abuse to a clergyperson, who responds by telling the women that some New Testament passage demands that they "submit" to their husbands because husbands are the "heads" of their wives. Some ministers quote biblical passages that suggest that the family unit is more sacred than the victim's life. Survivors are told that no matter how hellish the conditions are at home, they must never "break up" their families (though the victims are themselves being broken by their perpetrators). In many religious circles, pastors treat divorce far more harshly than they treat wife beating. This sanctification of the family and demonizing of divorce, coupled with the teaching of male headship and female submission, greatly increases the problem of domestic violence perpetrated against Christian women.

And this is exacerbated by "family values" sermons that blame women for all family and social ills. I once attended a service at an evangelical church at which more than five thousand worship every Sunday. The senior pastor began his homily by saying that we Americans have "lost our way." We once embraced strong Christian values, he said, but now our souls are wandering. The minister abruptly turned his comments from the entire family to women. "Women have forgotten their place," he shouted. "They want to do men's jobs, fight in the military, and even take over churches and their homes. But anyone who believes a woman is equal to a man must be a Ph.D. homosexual from California." The congregation loudly cheered the pastor's blatant bigotry. I never returned to that church.

Headship

Professor of New Testament David Scholer has observed a connection between the idea of "headship" and men's justification for the abuse of women. He notes, "The connection between abuse and the Bible appears to have at least two dimensions, especially within the various strands of the Christian tradition. First, many men who abuse their wives appear to feel that the alleged biblical teaching of 'male headship' is warrant, at least in some degree, for their behavior. Second, many abused women, especially those who have been taught the biblical principles of male headship and female submission, have understood the abuse they have received as either God's rightful punishment for their sins or God's will for their lives, even if it involves suffering unjustly."[15]

The Greek word *kephale,* often translated as "head," has a number of metaphorical uses in the New Testament. Ordinarily it denotes "source," "origin," or "preeminence," rather than "authority over" or "ruler." As Greek language scholar Catherine Clark Kroeger writes, "Let us be aware that a metaphor is just that—a figure of speech used to enforce a concept. Furthermore, metaphors may change meaning in different languages and cultures. In French, for instance, 'head' does not have the meaning of 'boss' or 'chief' as it does in English. In ancient Greek, the original language in which the New Testament was written, 'head' very seldom denoted a person in a position of power or superiority."[16]

In 1 Corinthians 11:11-12, Paul discusses the need for equality and mutuality between intimate partners. "Nevertheless, in the Lord woman is not independent of man or man independent of woman. For just as woman came from man, so man comes through woman; but all things come from God" (NRSV). The other place in the New Testament where *kephale* refers to the relationship between women and men is in Ephesians 5:21-33. In the first century, the general Jewish and Greco-Roman understanding of marriage was that wives were to submit to their husbands in all things. Ephesians 5:24 reads, "Just as the church is subject to Christ, so also wives ought to be, in everything, to their husbands" (NRSV). But as Scholer points out, "[I]t is clear that this cultural understanding of marriage is significantly qualified for those in Christ, so that the passage teaches an overarching concept of mutual submission. In this context, *kephale* hardly means 'authority over,' especially in the leadership and authority-bearing sense for husbands over wives given to it by so many of the traditionalist and complementarian interpreters."[17]

Another New Testament passage used by proponents of the male headship/female submission model is 1 Timothy 2:12: "I permit no woman to teach or to have authority over a man; she is to keep silent" (NRSV). When one studies this verse in the context of 1 Timothy 2:8-15, it quickly becomes apparent that the passage is addressing a problem of false teachers in the church. The verb used in verse 12, *authentein,* is very rare. In fact this is the only time it appears in the New Testament. In the classical Greek period, from the sixth to the fourth century B.C., the word carried with it the sense of a violent act, such as murder or suicide. Even during the period when the New Testament was written, *authentein* was associated with murder or a murderer.[18] In 1 Timothy 2:12, the verb refers to women "initiating" or "perpetrating" heretical teachings that 1 Timothy was written to oppose.[19] Scholer says, "I am convinced that the evidence . . . clearly establishes *authentein* as a negative term, indicating violence and inappropriate behavior. Thus, what Paul does not allow for women in 1 Timothy 2 is this type of behavior. Therefore, the text is not a transcultural, normative establishment of male headship and leadership with the concomitant view of female submission. I understand the impact of these further studies of *authentein* to support and establish more clearly the view I and many others have expressed that 1 Timothy 2 is opposing the negative behavior of women, probably the women mentioned in 1 Timothy 5:15 who follow and represent the false teachers 1 and 2 Timothy are dedicated to opposing."[20]

Submission

> *Why is it that an awful lot of pastors and perpetrators only read the sentence that says, 'Wives, submit yourselves to your husbands'? They even overlook the first verse that tells husbands and wives to submit themselves to one another.*
>
> —FATHER DAN SMITH, EPISCOPAL PRIEST, PASTOR OF ST. TIMOTHY'S EPISCOPAL CHURCH, WEST DES MOINES, IOWA

Many clergypeople teach that the Bible tells women to submit to their husbands but do not teach the numerous New Testament passages that instruct husbands to submit to their wives. I am amazed that these ministers do not recognize (or perhaps even care about) the damage caused by their lopsided viewpoint. Instructing wives that they are the only party that should submit in a marriage partnership sends the message that women are not only subordinates in the world, but also viewed less favorably by God. The teaching makes it much easier for husbands to batter their wives, feel excused for it, and blame their actions on the victims. Pastors must beware: this one-sided teaching about submission is dangerous and contradictory to the Bible.

The Greek word *hupotasso,* which is commonly translated as "submit," has several different meanings. In fact, there are a cluster of words commonly understood to be related to "submission" in the Greek New Testament: *hupotasso* (a verb meaning to submit, but also to behave responsibly toward another, to align oneself with, or to relate to another in a meaningful way); *hupotaktes* (an adjective meaning submissive, but more commonly, behaving in an orderly or proper fashion); *anupotaktos* (an adjective that is opposite to *hupotaktes:* disorderly, irresponsible, confused, or lacking meaning); and *hupotage* (a noun meaning submission, attachment, or copy).[21]

In Ephesians 5:21, *hupotasso* carries with it the idea of mutual support and responsibility: "Submit to one another out of reverence for Christ" (NIV). Then comes the most famous text quoted to women: "Wives, submit to your husbands as to the Lord" (Eph. 5:22 NIV). Catherine Clark Kroeger advises, "Non-Greek readers need to understand that this is not what the text says. There is no verb at all in verse 22. Instead, one must continue the sense of the verb found in verse 21, 'being subject to one another—wives to your own husbands.' Whatever 'submit' or 'be subject' means in verse 21 must also be its sense in verse 22—and in 21 it clearly implies mutuality."[22]

The evidence suggests that pastors and other spiritual leaders who insist that wives should submit to their husbands must also proclaim that the New Testament also instructs husbands to be subject to their wives:

> *The husband should fulfill his marital duty to his wife, and likewise the wife to her husband. The wife's body does not belong to her alone but also to her husband. In the same way, the husband's body does not belong to him alone but also to his wife. (1 Cor. 7:3-4 NIV)*

> *For you were called to freedom, brothers and sisters; only do not use your freedom as an opportunity for self-indulgence, but through love become slaves to one another. (Gal. 5:13 NRSV)*

> *Submit to one another out of reverence for Christ. (Eph. 5:21 NIV)*

Do nothing out of selfish ambition or vain conceit, but in humility consider others better than yourselves. (Phil. 2:3 NIV)

Isaiah 38:19

In October 1997, Mary Stewart Van Leeuwen, professor and resident scholar at the Center for Christian Women in Leadership at Eastern College in St. David's, Pennsylvania, heard Promise Keepers' CEO Bill McCartney proclaim on National Public Radio his position on male headship verses spousal equality in marriage. Van Leeuwen said McCartney took the same stand in August 1995 on the (then) *MacNeil-Lehrer News Hour*. What struck Van Leeuwen was the fact that McCartney did not use any of the New Testament passages we have just discussed, nor the passages in Genesis 2 and 3 we addressed earlier in this chapter. Instead, on both occasions Van Leeuwen quoted McCartney as saying, "Almighty God has mandated that the man take the spiritual lead in the home. Isaiah 38:19 says 'A *father* to the children shall make known the truth.'" Van Leeuwen said, "His emphasis made it clear that he saw this text as authorizing fathers to be responsible for mediating God's teaching to their children in a way that mothers are not." When the professor looked closely at the context of this verse herself she said, "What I found made me uncertain whether I should laugh or cry."[23]

It is important to mention Bill McCartney because he *is* a spiritual leader. Promise Keepers influences millions of men, instructing them on how they should act as husbands, fathers, and Christians. Therefore, it is McCartney's Christian responsibility to be accurate in his teachings about the Bible. This takes us back to Mary Stewart Van Leeuwen's closer look at Isaiah 38:19. After walking the reader through some background history of the book of Isaiah, the professor centers on chapter 38 verse 19, the second half of which is McCartney's proof-text for husbandly headship, albeit not quoted quite accurately: "The living, the living—they praise you, as I am doing today; fathers tell their children about your faithfulness." Five other translations, both Catholic and Protestant, are largely comparable to the New International Version, although the Revised English

Bible connects the two halves of the verse more explicitly by rendering it: "The living, only the living can confess you as I do this day my God, just as a father makes your faithfulness known to his sons."

Either way the message is clear: Hezekiah is grateful to God because while alive he can continue to praise God and teach God's ways to his children. In no way is this intended as a commentary on male spousal priority regarding the teaching of children, especially when we recall that the Pentateuch speaks consistently of the respect due to fathers and mothers alike, that both the Gospels and epistles reaffirm this teaching, and that the book of Proverbs exhorts its listeners at least half a dozen times to heed the specific teachings of mothers.[24]

Let me say again: it is vital that all clergy and other spiritual leaders be accurate in what they preach and teach women, men, and children about the Bible. Otherwise, it makes it very easy for perpetrators of violence to twist the Scriptures to justify their position on the ill-treatment of women (and on all other matters), and for women to feel that they deserve it.

Divorce

The sin that has come into a relationship resulting from an abusive partner cannot be denied. I can't say that I've ever advised or encouraged anyone to get a divorce. But there are times when I think it's understandable, and sometimes even when it may be necessary.

—REVEREND PATRICK HANDLSON, PRESBYTERIAN MINISTER AND PASTOR OF FIRST PRESBYTERIAN CHURCH (U.S.A.), HASTINGS, MINNESOTA

Many of the victims of domestic violence I interviewed while writing this book said they had been told by a Catholic priest or Protestant pastor that divorce, under any circumstance including domestic violence, was a sin and strictly prohibited by Scripture. Women need to stay in their marriages for the sake of the children, the sanctity of the family unit, and also to help "save" an abuser and make him "holy," the victims said clergy advised. Mary, a survivor whose story will be shared in greater detail in chapter 3, recalls her pastors' response to her twelve-year marriage to an abusive man: "I remember the ministers at church telling me how much God hates divorce and that divorce was a sin. If I divorced my husband, they said I would be in the wrong. So, even after all the years of his abuse, I had this major guilt when I finally left him. I still felt that I was the bad guy because I initiated the separation."

Another survivor, Debra, who will also share more of her story with us in chapter 3, recalled the strong feelings of guilt she experienced after the dissolution of her eighteen-year marriage to an abusive husband (even though he was unfaithful to her and initiated the divorce proceedings). "One night I asked a minister to please pray for and with me," remembered Debra. "It was one of those times that I felt I was losing my mind. I told the minister I didn't want to see my husband anymore. I could not continue to put myself in that harmful situation, I said. But the minister told me that I needed to go back to William and, maybe, I could lead him to the Lord. The minister's words nearly killed me."

What do the Scriptures actually teach about divorce? Are there any circumstances when divorce is permissible? How have the views held by some clergypeople about divorce contributed to keeping victims of domestic violence in dangerous marriages?

The Christian Scriptures offer two circumstances under which divorce is approved. Let us first consider the verses cited from the Gospel of Matthew:

> But I say to you that anyone who divorces his wife, except on the grounds of unchastity, causes her to commit adultery; and whoever marries a divorced woman commits adultery. (Matthew 5:32 NRSV)

> And I say to you, whoever divorces his wife, except for unchastity, and marries another commits adultery. (Matthew 19:9 NRSV)

The Greek word *porneia,* translated in the New Revised Standard Version as "unchastity," is rendered in other translations as "unfaithfulness" or "immorality." In a paper addressing the biblical concessions for divorce, Catherine Clark Kroeger writes, "This word *[porneia]* can mean any sort of inappropriate sexual attitude or action, whether fornication, adultery, prostitution, or sexual abuse."[25]

Craig S. Keener, a New Testament professor, translates *porneia* as "immorality." "This term implies any sort of sexual sin, except when the context designates a particular kind; and the context here fails to narrow the meaning of 'immorality' down in any way. 'Immorality' here is not just premarital sex, nor is it just incest; it is any kind of sexual unfaithfulness to one's current spouse. Since the kind of unfaithfulness normally perpetrated by people already married is adultery, the kind of immorality that would most often be implied here is adultery."[26]

The second concession to the scriptural teachings about divorce is offered by the Apostle Paul:

> To the married I give this command—not I but the Lord—that the wife should not separate from her husband (but if she does separate, let her remain unmarried or else be reconciled to her husband), and that the husband should not divorce his wife.
>
> To the rest I say—I and not the Lord—that if any believer has a wife who is an unbeliever, and she consents to live with him, he should not divorce her. And if any woman has a husband who is an unbeliever, and he consents to live with her, she should not divorce him. For the unbelieving husband is made holy through his wife, and the unbelieving wife is made holy through her husband. Otherwise, your children would be unclean, but as it is, they are holy. But if the unbelieving partner separates, let it be so; in such a case the brother or sister is not bound. It is to peace that God has called you. Wife, for all you know, you might save your husband. Husband, for all you know, you might save your wife. (1 Cor. 7:10-16 NRSV)

Religiously mixed marriages were common in Corinth in Paul's day. Many first-generation Christians were married before they became Christians and converted out of paganism. Now that they found themselves in a marriage with a spiritually incompatible husband or wife, what were they to do? Paul's answer is that the believer should stay with the unbeliever unless the unbeliever is the one who dissolves the marriage covenant by leaving (7:10-13).[27]

But what does desertion involve? A biblical scholar notes that even though an unbelieving spouse could give love and respect, and honor a marriage by being faithful to it, some nonbelievers in

Corinth were unfaithful to their spouses. "It is not the mate's passive unbelief that makes the marriage unsettled but rather an active unbelief expressed in the will to disrupt the union, presumably on either religious or personal grounds," asserts James Earl Massey. "We can assume that in Corinth some non-Christian partners were involved in extramarital affairs; indeed, that some, as devotees to pagan religious practices, excused their actions on religious grounds. Without overt reference to this kind of situation Paul ruled that the Christian partner was free if the unbelieving mate quit the marriage. The use of *apistos* was likely a subtle reference to the deserting unbeliever's untrustworthiness as a mate."[28] (The Greek word *apistos* is used several times in 1 Corinthians 7 [verses 12, 13, 14, and 15]. In all instances, it is a term meaning one who is not a believer. Massey suggests that because of opposing beliefs, *apistos* also conveys a person who "is not trustworthy; in short, one who is not faithful.")[29]

First Corinthians then is attempting to bring a peaceful resolution to a troubled conflict involving matters of faith and practice. "This passage is well worth considering, especially in situations where all the conventional aspects of marriage have been lost, whether through infidelity, desertion, or abuse," maintains Catherine Clark Kroeger. "A marriage of abuse cannot be a marriage reflecting Christ's love for the church. Paul comments 'a sister or brother is not bound in such circumstances.' *Douleuo,* the word translated as 'bound' literally means to serve in bondage as a slave. We might translate 'a sister or brother is not held in a bondage in such circumstances, for God has called you to peace' [1 Cor. 7:15]. It is that peace that must be prayerfully considered."[30]

The exception clause in Matthew 5:32 and 19:9 and Paul's added concession in 1 Corinthians 7:10-16 serve as a beacon of light to help clergy address more accurately the matter of divorce in marriages where abuse is present. In cases of domestic violence, the sacred vow of marriage, the chastity and "oneness" in God, is broken *not* by the victimized wife, but by her abusing husband. Many clergy erroneously blame the wife for leaving her spouse. In reality, the batterer destroyed the marriage covenant when he chose to abuse his wife. In essence he "deserted" her whether or not he remains in the home—by his inappropriate emotional, psychological, and sexual behavior. Still, often women are told by clergypeople that they must remain in an abusive marriage or, if they decide to leave, they must stay single for the rest of their lives. (Which is exactly what a second minister told Debra. Despite her husband's marital unfaithfulness and his desertion of the marriage to begin an intimate relationship with another woman, the pastor told Debra she could never remarry. "I didn't go back to that minister again," Debra lamented.)

Marriage is sacred, but so is the individual whom God created in God's own image—female as well as male. Only when both intimate partners commit to the biblical virtues of love and respect will a marriage be sustained and grow. Spousal abuse is not of God; it breaks apart women and families. Therefore, it is irresponsible for clergy to pressure women into remaining in marriages that pose danger to women and children who are battered by abusive husbands.

Conclusion

The practice of encouraging and excusing abusive and violent behavior perpetuated by men against women has been a part of the world since the beginning of time. Men who have beaten, raped, stalked, and murdered their wives and girlfriends have gotten away with these crimes without so much as a slap on the hands. Conversely, women have not only had to endure this brutality, but have also had to suffer the added emotional, psychological, and spiritual oppression of being blamed for their own victimization.

For the most part clergy have hindered rather than helped women break free from their abusive partners. Our apathy, denial, exhortations, ignorance, and misinterpretations of the Bible have added to women's pain and suffering and placed them in even greater danger. The time is long overdue for us pastors to stop turning our backs on domestic violence and begin speaking out against this sin. We have a duty to provide comfort and safety to victims and their children, to confront perpetrators with their inappropriate behavior, and to strongly encourage them to seek professional help for their violent actions. We have a responsibility to preach and teach the biblical truths about God's love, which binds women and men together as equals rather than ordering them in a hierarchy. As long as we refuse to fully carry out our pastoral duties, victims of domestic violence will continue to crumble emotionally, psychologically, and spiritually underneath the weight of brutality and scriptural misinterpretations, which no human deserves.

Questions for Discussion

1. What are the similarities and differences in the stories of creation told in Genesis 1 and 2? Discuss the role played by both man and woman in the temptation story found in Genesis 3:1-7.

2. Name several metaphorical uses of the Greek word *kephale*. Discuss how the different renderings can be helpful and harmful to women. Do the same for the Greek terms *hupotasso* and *authentein*.

3. What specific instructions are husbands given regarding how they should treat their wives in 1 Corinthians 7:3-4, Galatians 5:13, Ephesians 5:21 and 25-33, and Philippians 2:3?

4. Even if you are opposed to divorce, name at least three reasons why it is dangerous to pressure a victim of domestic violence to stay in an abusive marriage. What is the abuser's role/responsibility in the breakdown of a marriage? Discuss the exceptions given in which divorce is approved in Matthew 5:32 and 19:9, and in 1 Corinthians 7:10-16.

5. Discuss at least four possibly negative outcomes resulting from the male headship/female submission model in a marriage or intimate partnership.

6. Discuss several negative ramifications resulting from clergy's refusal to address the problem of domestic violence from pulpits, in classrooms, and in the community.

Chapter 2. Violence against Women: Separating Fact from Myth

I think the biggest myth still hanging around is that a woman can leave [an abusive relationship] if she wants to. This idea spins off other myths, such as: if she doesn't leave then maybe she likes being abused; maybe her relationship isn't as bad as she says it is; maybe she's just exaggerating; or, maybe things would improve if she would just change her behavior. None of these [myths] of course are true. Women don't leave for a variety of reasons, but one of the most important is that leaving doesn't stop the violence.

—DR. LENORE WALKER, PSYCHOLOGIST

Kara's Visit with Two Pastors[1]

Kara has been married to her husband, Rich, for sixteen years. Devout Christians, they both attend church regularly. Kara and Rich have a teenage son, and Kara describes her husband and son as "the great loves of my life."

Despite Kara's deep love for her husband, she told a coworker that Rich has abused her throughout their marriage. The disclosure was prompted by an incident that had occurred the week before. "I'd overcooked Rich's steak," Kara explained to her coworker. "It was so stupid of me; I can't do anything right. After sixteen years of marriage, you'd think a wife would know that her husband likes his meat medium rare, not well done." According to Kara, Rich then called her a "fat, stupid whore," threw the steak

47

in the trash, and left home to eat supper at a nearby restaurant. On other occasions, Kara said Rich derided her for being overweight, telling her he'd rather "screw a dog" than have sex with "a fat-ass pig" like her. Kara revealed that Rich also had pushed, slapped, and spit on her from time to time. Her husband's actions and words hurt deeply, she admitted. Still, Kara blamed herself for Rich's behavior.

"It's all my fault," she lamented. "If I were a better wife, if I weren't overweight and so stupid, Rich would have no need to say and do such awful things to me. Besides, he always apologizes for the bad mood he says I put him in and, afterwards, buys me orchids and takes me out to a nice dinner. He says that as a Christian wife I must forgive him." Rich also prefers not to treat her the way he does, Kara told the coworker, but says it is his "Christian duty to take authority" over her and to "correct" her when she is wrong. "My husband tells me the Bible demands that a man rule over his wife," Kara explained. "So when I'm out of line or do stupid things, then Rich has to put me in my place. Otherwise, my husband says, he's not truly a man of God."

Kara's coworker encouraged her to seek help from a professional trained to address situations of domestic violence. The coworker also recommended that Kara speak to someone who understood what the Bible actually teaches regarding how a man and woman should treat each other in marriage. The battered wife was reluctant to follow up on either suggestion. The day after Rich threw his overcooked steak in the trash, Kara explained, she went to see a male pastor who is also a counselor at a Christian counseling center. This minister told Kara "any woman who stays with a man who abuses her must either like being abused or she must be exaggerating her claims." The pastor also urged Kara to bring her husband to the next counseling session. "This will allow me to determine who's telling the truth," Kara said the minister told her.

The coworker asked Kara if she had sought help from her own pastor. Kara said she hadn't. Pastor Lee was loving and sensitive, but Kara feared that the minister's close relationship with her husband would bias him. "The pastor may side with Rich," Kara worried, "because my husband always presents himself as being this loving and respectful Christian leader around other people. Or, like that Christian counselor, Rev. Lee might think I either like being abused or I'm exaggerating."

Afraid, and yet needing emotional and spiritual guidance, Kara decided to confide in her pastor. Fortunately, Pastor Lee had taken some domestic violence training. Meeting with Kara at the church, the pastor told his battered parishioner that she had not done anything to deserve the abuse Rich was inflicting upon her. Domestic violence has nothing to do with whether or not a woman is a good wife, Christian, or cook; nor does it have anything to do with a woman's weight, intellectual capacity, or her either exaggerating or liking abuse. No one deserves to be victimized, the minister insisted. He also assured Kara that God loves her exactly the way she is.

Separating Fact from Myth

With appropriate training, clergy and other pastoral ministers can provide effective and sensitive spiritual support to victims of domestic abuse, as did Pastor Lee to Kara in the above story. Without this training, however, we are prone to offer poor and insensitive pastoral care, as did the minister Kara saw at the Christian counseling center. His response to Kara's disclosure was based on three common myths about abused women: women "like" being abused; they always exaggerate their claims of abuse; and women always lie about being abused. None of the myths is true. Nevertheless, these and countless other fictions are passed on from generation to generation as fact.

There are many false beliefs about domestic violence. Here I will examine the four most frequently mentioned myths cited by the clergy members I interviewed for this book. I will begin with the one that was, by far, stated the most often.

Myth #1: There are no abused women in my congregation.

Twelve million women in the United States—a staggering 25 percent of all American women—will be abused by an intimate partner. An estimated two million women in this country are assaulted by an intimate partner every year. The actual numbers are probably much higher because victims often remain silent, fearing both the stigma associated with abuse and the threat of further violence from the perpetrators.[2] Battered women also fear the type of responses they are likely to get from their pastors if they do disclose abuse. In addition, according to the Bureau of Justice Statistics, "intimate violence" is primarily a crime against women. In 1996, three of every four victims of intimate murder and 85 percent of victims of nonlethal intimate violence were female. The vast majority of abusers are adult or teenage males.[3]

Despite these mind-boggling figures, many of the 158 clergypeople I interviewed, especially the men, nonetheless insisted that there were no abused women worshiping in their congregations. Further, more than thirty other pastors, once again the vast majority of them men, declined my request for an interview because, according to them, there was simply no evidence of domestic violence within their churches. How can so many pastors be so blind to a problem that is staring them right in the face? Let's take a close look at three factors: denial, fear, and lack of domestic violence training. Each will be discussed at length in this book.

Denial

Clergypeople who told me there were no victims of domestic violence in their congregations based this hypothesis on one of two criteria. First, because no woman had ever disclosed an episode of abuse to these pastors, it must not be occurring. (A similar conclusion is made by Pastor Carl in the preceding chapter in "Rita's Story.") None of these (mostly male) clergy associated the lack of disclosure with *their* lack of speaking about domestic violence in prayers, sermons, Sunday school classes, and so forth. They responded coldly to my suggestion that they consider including a word about abuse during some aspect of their midweek and Sunday services. When I interviewed the pastor of a large congregation located in an affluent Midwestern suburb at his church office, he praised me for addressing a problem that is, in his words, "threatening the very existence of mankind." Domestic violence is a "plague on the soul of man," he said. But the spiritual leader quickly added that he would have little to contribute to my book because, fortunately, his parish was "abuse free." The seven hundred men and women who worship in the congregation on a regular basis are "far too progressive and sophisticated" to get caught in "a web of destruction and evil that results from domestic violence," the pastor insisted.

I asked the minister how often he addressed the topic of violence against women, either in sermons, teachings, or pastoral prayers. I also inquired if he had ever placed a statement on the bulletin board in the church narthex or in the Sunday morning bulletin condemning domestic violence. The pastor's response chilled me. "There's no need for such activities here," he snapped. "Why address a subject that's a non-issue?" Turning abruptly to the bookcase behind his chair, the pastor took an 8-by-10-inch cross-stitched plaque off the shelf and handed it to me. It read, "Not in This Church." This was the motto by which he and the members of his congregation lived, he said. "We simply don't tolerate the ill-treatment of women or the badgering of any other of God's creatures here," the minister insisted. "I often remind my people of one fact: if they have negative attitudes or are controlled by any kind of bigotry, then they need to worship elsewhere. We won't stand for such evil behavior—not in this church."

I heard a very different message from this motto than the pastor perhaps intended. If I were a member of his parish, I said, and were a victim of domestic violence or some other catastrophic problem, I would hesitate to disclose it to him or anyone else who embraced this motto. "Not in This Church," I explained, could sound like "I don't know and don't care to hear about any complicated or messy problems."

The pastor did not receive my point of view well. "I don't know what in the hell kind of book you're writing," he shouted as he stood up and walked toward the door, "but I can guarantee you that such bullshit will not be read by me or any of my parishioners." The minister then dismissed me from his office.

Women pastors are not necessarily more responsive to the problem than men. Although many of the female clergy I interviewed didn't deny that abused women were among their parishioners, these pastors minimized their responsibility to victims. As I will discuss further in chapter 6, a number of women pastors told me that because most of the perpetrators of domestic violence are men, it's up to male pastors and other men to "fix the problem." When I challenged them to give me specifics on how the women clergy themselves are addressing the problem of domestic violence, very few could offer anything concrete. For example, a clergywoman serving a well-to-do parish in Connecticut told me that female pastors had to do "hardly anything" to show battered women how much they care for them. "Victims know, intuitively, that clergywomen are concerned about their well-being," claimed the pastor. When I pressed this minister to give me some examples of her pastoral care to victims that went beyond intuition, she became upset. "As a man, you wouldn't understand the examples even if I gave them to you," she retorted. Maybe. But, like many of our male colleagues, I suspect that this particular Christian leader did not offer me any specific pastoral care approaches for victims because she is not practicing any.

Many of the women pastors I interviewed also tended to judge victims by their own standards. Several abused women told me that they found this approach unhelpful. "Women clergy can be just as judgmental and inappropriate as males," asserts Julie Owens, an abuse survivor and the executive director of an agency that educates and trains service providers—doctors, nurses, psychologists, police officers, pastors—on how to identify, treat, and refer victims. Owens is very troubled about clergypeople who either deny the existence of victims in their congregations or blame victims for their abuse. "Women clergy members say, 'I wouldn't put up with that. The first time somebody hit me, I'd be out of there.' These statements imply to the victim that she is somehow responsible for perpetuating, allowing, or stopping the abuse. None of this is true."

Many clergypeople I interviewed (again, most were men) supported their hypothesis that none of their congregants were abused women by reciting the myth of the ideal Christian man. No true man of God would ever use coercion, force, or manipulation to control his wife or girlfriend, male pastors repeatedly told me. When Christ is at the center of a household, explained one pastor, then violence is simply not "in the heart of a man." This myth of the ideal Christian man, who rises above the messages most males hear their entire lives about power, control, and violence, sustains the larger myth that there are no abused women worshiping in Christian congregations. As a result, scores of Christian women who are being battered by their husbands or boyfriends (many of whom are worshiping in our churches) suffer in silence, all alone.

Fear
Many pastors choose to believe that there are no abused women in their congregations because of fear (rather than to face the fact that victims are everywhere). If we admit there are in fact women in our pews who are being battered, then we are forced to deal with this pervasive problem. "Pastors don't want to take on the responsibility of caring for victims," states Rev. John Tschudy, pastor of the St. John's United Church of Christ in Slinger, Wisconsin. "Every congregation, large or small, has women who are being abused sitting in its pews. But, out of fear of saying or doing the wrong things, many pastors deny that the problem even exists in their own churches."

A ministerial colleague named Steve asked me to speak at his parish one Sunday morning while he was away. Pastor Steve told me he had been preaching a series of sermons on how the Bible instructs women and men to practice egalitarianism in marriage. Keeping with this theme, I informed the minister that I would speak on the topic of domestic violence. My text, I said, would be drawn from the very same verses that have been used for centuries to justify the subjugation of women and the dominance of men: Ephesians 5:21-33. Steve welcomed my sermon choice. In fact, he shared that only a few weeks earlier he himself had also preached from the very same text. "Christians need to hear the message about equality among husbands and wives several times a year," he asserted.

My sermon was received warmly by the members of Steve's congregation. As is always the case when I preach or teach about domestic violence, several women afterwards disclosed personal stories of being abused by an intimate or former intimate male partner. Both Steve and his parishioners extended an open invitation for me to come back and speak at the church in the future.

The pastor of another local parish heard about this sermon from one of his female parishioners who had visited Steve's church the Sunday I spoke. "You opened up a huge can of worms," said the minister when he phoned me five days after the service. "I've pastored this church for more than six years," he continued in a very loud tone, "but until this week no woman had ever brought up to me the issue of being abused by her husband. The woman from my church who attended your service is a wonderful Christian wife and mother. She has never made waves. But your sermon agitated her. She now claims her husband, who is one of the finest Christian men I've ever known, has been abusing her for years." According to this pastor, my sermon also caused other women worshiping in his congregation to "fall away from the truth." The spiritual leader tried to explain to me what this phrase meant. "The parishioner who attended your sermon has now riled several other so-called victims worshiping in my congregation," the pastor lamented. "They tried to tell me about their own Christian husbands abusing them. The women want to begin a support group for abuse victims and they asked to hold the meetings in the church on Saturdays. They even requested that I begin speaking about domestic violence from the pulpit. Why couldn't you have just left well enough alone?"

Unfortunately, this disgruntled colleague is not the first nor the last clergy member to criticize my preaching and teaching about domestic violence in churches. One of the primary reasons these pastors encourage me to drop the subject is, I believe, fear.

"Domestic violence evokes fear in many professionals, especially those who are ill-prepared to deal with it," asserted Yvonne Yim, a clinical social worker at The Queen's Medical Center in Honolulu.

Actively involved in the domestic violence movement for several years, Yim, a Christian, offers pastors educational programs on domestic violence. Few male clergy have taken the training. "Many male ministers have said, 'Well, domestic abuse doesn't happen in this parish, but if it ever does occur, we'll get back to you.' Other clergy tell me they don't want to open up a can of worms. 'Let's not rock the boat', they say. 'I'm not ready to deal with that issue quite yet.' While these pastors remain stuck in denial and fear, the abuse of Christian women continues."

Yes, if pastors begin to admit that victims worship among us; if in our sermons, classrooms, and prayers we identify domestic violence as a morally reprehensible act, then victims will come out in droves to seek our support. Is this the so-called "can of worms" many ministers are afraid of opening? Why?

In chapter 6 we will explore in detail the story of Robert S. Owens, Jr., a retired Presbyterian (U.S.A.) minister. By his own admission, Rev. Robert Owens spent the first three decades of his ministry avoiding the issue of domestic violence. Then he discovered that his own daughter had married an abuser. After Owens and his daughter survived a brutal knife attack by his son-in-law, the pastor received domestic violence training and began speaking out against abuse. The response from women in his church was dramatic. "Victims started making appointments with me almost immediately," the minister said. "And they never stopped coming."

How can we ease our fears and, like Robert Owens, become spokespersons against domestic violence? First, we pastors must get proper domestic violence training. Although education will not remove all of our anxieties or make the abuse itself less complicated to deal with, it will allow ministers to become effective and sensitive caregivers to victims. Training is vital. As we will see below, without this training pastors will remain in the dark about all the suffering faced by victims in our midst.

Lack of Domestic Violence Training
Because so many clergy lack training, they do not understand that domestic abuse is not just physical violence. It can take many forms,

including physical battering, sexual battering, property and pet destruction, and emotional abuse/psychological battering. As I will discuss in chapter 4, most clergypeople perceive domestic violence as only those sensational cases of physical assault that get reported in the media: severe beatings, burnings, chokings, shootings, stabbings, murders. My clergy colleagues tended to overlook the more subtle acts of physical violence that men perpetrate against women, such as pushing, shoving, slapping, or spitting on them. Pastors tended also to understand sexual battering only as forced sexual intercourse. Even then, several male clergy said they did not understand how any husband could ever be accused of raping his wife. The other two forms of abuse that were discussed, property or pet destruction and emotional abuse/psychological battering, were identified only by a small number of well trained clergy, the vast majority of them women. The point is, if ministers cannot even identify the forms of domestic violence, then it's no wonder that many of them believe there are no abused women worshiping in their congregations.

A lack of domestic violence training causes some pastors to treat episodes of abuse as a "private matter between a married couple." Recall the words of Pastor Carl in chapter 1. After a long-term parishioner named Rita had disclosed countless acts of violence perpetrated against her by Walt, her husband of fifteen years, and even though I myself told Pastor Carl about one episode of abuse I inadvertently witnessed over the telephone, the minister dismissed the violence as simply a "private spat" that all intimate couples experience from time to time. "I understand you unfortunately overheard a private spat between a husband and wife," Pastor Carl said to me in his office two days after the abuse. "Hell, married life is tough; every couple has arguments."

Pastors who think domestic violence is like any argument all intimate couples experience from time to time are likely to engage in a very dangerous practice: counseling victims of domestic violence with their offenders. Bringing a couple together for counseling under these circumstances is always risky. Some pastors said they bring the couple in for counseling to "get at the truth" or to "weed out the liar." The minister whom Kara saw at the Christian counseling center sought to do the former. I find revealing the fact that no clergy member has told me he has asked a man who is sharing some aspect of his life to bring in his female partner in order for the pastor to "get at the truth" or "weed out the liar." Why not? The vast majority of pastors I interviewed said they bring a victimized woman together with her offender in a sincere effort to help both people "work things out." But spiritual leaders must take heed: counseling a woman together with her perpetrator is extremely risky for the victim. This practice could lead to her suffering further abuse, even death. "In my own experience, not only did a year of couples counseling fail to help the relationship, I feel that it actually made things worse," recalled Julie Owens. "My husband and I saw a (Ph.D.) psychologist one to two times a week over the period of one year, after a long trial separation period due to his constant verbal and emotional abuse of me. During this unsuccessful reconciliation attempt, we were renting an apartment in my family's home, and my family was very supportive of me. In the time we were under her care, the therapist made two near-fatal mistakes, which she now admits and regrets. The first was not labeling the primary problem (violence), and the other was never assessing my husband's high level of lethality and dangerousness."[4]

Psychologists Neil Jacobson and John Gottman, in their book *When Men Batter Women,* write: "[C]ouples therapy makes little sense as a first-line treatment. One would not expect couples therapy to stop the violence, since the violence is not about things that the women are doing or saying. Couples therapy has other disadvantages. First, it can increase the risk of violence by forcing couples to deal with conflict on a weekly basis, leaving the batterer in a constant state of readiness to batter. Second, when the couple is seen together, the therapist implies that they are mutually responsible for the violence. This implication is handy for the batterer, since it supports his point of view: 'If she would just change her behavior, the violence would stop.' The victim ends up being blamed for her own victimization."[5]

Again, abused women are found everywhere—including in our congregations. If ministers are going to provide effective care to these women, we must first recognize this fact. Second, we ministers must acknowledge that the violence perpetrated by men against their female intimate partners is far more than just the normal arguments couples experience from time to time—more than a "private spat" or a "lovers' quarrel"—and far too complicated for us to attempt to handle alone. Abusers need the help of professionals trained in offender-specific interventions. Victims need assistance from people qualified to deal with the various dynamics of abuse. Most ministers do not have training in either of these areas. Even if we did, it would still be very dangerous for us to bring a victim together with her batterer in a counseling session when domestic violence is suspected in the relationship.

Myth #2: Christian survivors need only faith, prayer, a positive attitude, and God to be freed from domestic violence.

Joel said he didn't understand all the fuss. Sure, women had been abused in the past by the men who claimed to love them, but, at the dawn of a new millennium, wives and girlfriends have never had it so good. Besides, women aren't the only group to be oppressed. Look at blacks, Indians, Jews—even the people from his Scandinavian heritage. His ancestors had to endure cramped quarters and rough seas on their journey to the New World, he explained. Even after arriving in America, they were derided for their appearance, customs, and speech, and were forced to live in ghetto-like conditions. But they overcame these obstacles and began to make positive contributions to society. Women could do the same if they stopped feeling sorry for themselves. "Leave the past in the past and thank God for all the blessings," was Joel's advice to battered women. "Acting like victims will keep them victims for life."

What type of person harbors the kind of views just described? Is Joel living on a remote part of the earth unable to access the endless amount of data available at the click of a mouse? Or, could he even be from another planet or a different galaxy? Perhaps. But Joel is not an alien. He is the senior pastor of a large evangelical church located in the Midwest.[6]

The misconception that Christian victims of domestic violence can somehow be freed by faith, prayer, a positive attitude, and a stronger belief in God has forced many abused women to remain in unhealthy and potentially lethal relationships with violent men. "I've become convinced of the link between domestic abuse and beliefs that are commonly preached and taught in churches," asserts the Rev. John Tschudy. "When ministers tell women they have to pray harder, submit totally to their husbands and have to somehow show more faith in God, then we give victims the impression that they are to blame for their own abuse. This makes it even harder for them to disclose or leave a violent situation, and more difficult for victims to react against the abuse in any way."

Debbie Hauhio, a victim advocate for the Family Advocacy Program at Marine Corps Base Hawaii in Kaneohe Bay, also notes a link between what Christian victims hear from their pastors and how these women feel forced to stay in unhealthy marriages. "I once had a Christian woman tell me she had to stay in an abusive relationship because her pastor said, despite the violence, it was the woman's duty to try to make the marriage work," Hauhio recalled. A Christian herself, Hauhio expressed disappointment at the poor care victims may receive from male pastors. "These women respect their ministers as men of God. So when pastors tell them to stay in violent marriages, victims feel they have no other choice but to put up with the abuse their husbands are perpetrating."

Trite phrases that clergypeople offer abused women can make life worse for victims. Couched as sound spiritual advice, statements like the following blame abused women for their own victimization and keep them imprisoned in dangerous relationships. Therefore, these platitudes must absolutely be avoided:

• Stop feeling sorry for yourself.
• Leave the past in the past and thank God for all of your blessings.
• God will never give you more than you can handle.
• All Christians have crosses to bear.

- A bad husband (father) is better than no husband (father).
- Although the abuse is terrible, it'll make you a much stronger Christian.
- Submit yourself totally to the will of your husband and then the abuse will stop.
- Go back to your husband and pray for a miracle.
- God calls us to be a living sacrifice.
- You have to work harder at being a good wife (or mother, sexual partner, etc.).
- Suffering builds character.
- Your faith in God will turn this negative experience into a positive outcome. It will save your marriage.
- Confess your sins and pray harder.

These platitudes work against effective and sensitive pastoral care to victims of domestic violence, as does the myth that Christian survivors need only faith, prayer, a positive attitude, and God to be freed from violent men. These assertions only blame victims for the violence perpetrated against them. As spiritual leaders we must be willing to get the education and training we need to help us understand all the complex dynamics associated with violence against women by intimate male partners. We must then be willing to minister to these hurting women diligently, resisting the temptation to use empty phrases in an attempt to rush them through the usually long-term process of grief and healing.

Myth #3: Domestic violence occurs only in certain cultural, racial, and socioeconomic groups, and only in urban areas.

An article in *The Christian Ministry* tells the story of a woman named Betty. She had it all: a managerial position in a prestigious company, a daughter and son attending Ivy League schools, a home that was paid for, and the directorship of the largest church choir in the state. Betty also had a husband who abused her all twenty-six years of their marriage.[7]

I often use Betty's story in pastoral care workshops on domestic violence. At the beginning of these sessions, I ask clergy and lay leaders to read the entire two-page article in which Betty is featured. Then I request the group to offer a description of this battered woman: her age, countenance, moods, even her race. I explain upfront that there are a host of myths and stereotypes associated with abused women. This opening discussion, I contend, will help us to become more sensitive to the needs of these hurting women.

Although the first page of *The Christian Ministry* article is illustrated by a large graphic of a white female figure with long, black hair, crouched in a fetal position, most white workshop participants identify Betty as African American, Filipina, Hawaiian, Hispanic, Latina, Native American, or Samoan. Asking white individuals why so few of them assumed Betty was white has evoked responses that teeter on the bizarre. To cite just a few:

- Betty sounds like a Hispanic name.
- I thought the article said that Betty is black. (It doesn't.)
- The figure in the graphic looks like an Indian woman.
- The article says Betty is overweight. Many black, Hawaiian, and Samoan women have weight problems.
- Filipino and Latino cultures condone domestic violence. White cultures don't.
- I've never had a white woman tell me she was a victim of abuse. (When I asked this particular pastor if women from any other culture had ever disclosed abuse to him, he reluctantly said they had not.)
- Women from minority races are abused more frequently than white women, I think.

In truth, domestic violence occurs among all cultures, races, and socioeconomic groups, and in rural as well as urban areas. It is critical for clergy and other ministers to recognize this fact. If we do not, we will not be able to provide effective and practical spiritual care to the victims worshiping in our own congregations. However, an alarming number of white male and even a few white female pastors told me that domestic violence was "not present" in their communities. Some of these same spiritual leaders recommended that I go to other areas of their respective cities to gather my data. In every instance, I later discovered that these "other areas" were inhabited either by minority races or by poor whites. One white pastor in Alabama told me if I wanted to discover the "root source" of domestic violence in his state, I needed to concentrate on what he called the "black-belt communities." I'd find the people there, he said, who would more likely be involved in wife abuse: "poor, uneducated, and unemployed black men."

Let us then focus our attention on the factors that contribute to many clergypeople believing the myth that victims (and perpetrators) of domestic violence are found only among certain cultural, racial, and socioeconomic groups, and only in urban areas. We'll begin with the first segment of this myth.

Domestic violence is found only among certain cultural, racial, and socioeconomic groups.
The American Medical Association (AMA) says conservative studies indicate that two million women are assaulted by their partners each year, but experts believe that the true incidence of partner violence is probably closer to four million per year. Further, the AMA states that 30 percent of American women report they have been physically abused by their husband or boyfriend at one time or another.[8] In addition, according to the Bureau of Justice Statistics National Crime Victimization Survey (August 1995), women of all races are equally vulnerable to attacks by intimates.[9] Despite these statistics many clergypeople, as well as individuals from the general public, continue to embrace the myth that domestic violence is found only among certain cultural, racial, and socioeconomic groups.

"There are many myths and stereotypes about Latinos that are held by Catholic priests and other people in the religious community, as well as by folks in the general public," said Bertha Herrera, who serves as the community liaison and domestic violence advocate at Venice Family Clinic in Venice, California. Ninety percent of the battered women at the clinic are Latina. "People seem to think just because someone is poor or lacking education that domestic violence happens more frequently with them. But abuse occurs among the rich as well as the poor, and among the people who are highly educated as well as among those people who have little or no education. Yes, there are a great number of myths and stereotypes placed on the Latina community when, in fact, we know that domestic violence crosses all cultural and social borders."

Shortly after reading an article on domestic violence I had written for *Leadership* journal (Spring 1999), a colleague, let's call her Wanda, came to see me in my office. A Christian and highly respected physician, Wanda has practiced medicine in Honolulu for several years. "I've been abused by my husband throughout our eight-year marriage," confessed Wanda matter-of-factly. "Just like the woman in *Leadership*, I've been forced by my husband to keep a daily log of all my activities, been stripped of all my credit cards, and I've been called names a Christian man shouldn't even call a cockroach. I've also been kicked, punched, and raped by this so-called man of God. My husband tells me this is his right. As a Christian man and head of our household, he says, the Bible tells him to do whatever's necessary to keep me in line; and he insists I need to obey him no matter what."

Wanda tried to tell her parish pastor, a white male, about the abuse. But the minister's initial response turned her off. "My pastor told me 'Wanda, you're a beautiful *haole* lady. [*Haole* is a Hawaiian word many of the islanders use to describe white people.] You are an intelligent physician making more than six figures a year. I refuse to believe you'd put up with abuse, as though you were stupid, a minority, or poor.'" Wanda told me she would never again discuss the abuse with her pastor.

The above incident is consistent with the responses I receive when I use "Betty's Story" at pastoral care workshops. A number of white ministers, especially white males, believe the myth that domestic violence occurs primarily among poor and uneducated folks from minority cultural and racial backgrounds. Curiously, even the three Hispanic and two African American male ministers I interviewed, all of whom are pastoring predominantly white parishes, also told me that domestic violence is not a problem in their churches or communities. "When I lived in the inner city, women were beaten all the time," declared an African American pastor serving an affluent, predominantly white parish in the Pacific Northwest. "But here folks don't get involved in that mess."

I am deeply troubled by these assumptions. When clergypeople embrace the myth that abuse occurs only in certain groups and communities, it prevents them from providing pastoral care to abused women who do not fit into their stereotype. Thus Wanda and other attractive, intelligent, and rich white victims worshiping in these congregations will continue to receive ineffective care from their pastors. Belief in this myth also raises several critical questions; for instance: Who in the parish is providing the proper spiritual care to attractive, intelligent, and rich white abused women? Do pastors think that all abused women who fit this description are either lying or stupid? Why did Wanda's minister even mention her physical appearance, intelligence, race, and socioeconomic status? What do these qualities have to do with domestic violence? Is the pastor implying that it's OK to abuse women who are less attractive, poor, uneducated, and from a minority culture or race?

I believe that so many of the male pastors I interviewed who are serving well-to-do and predominantly white congregations assume that domestic violence does not happen in their particular churches or communities because this assumption allows these pastors to avoid caring for the victims in their midst. "I sure wish I could help you out in this important study, but we just don't have the kinds of women you need for your book," said one male pastor serving an upper-class white parish in the Midwest. Interviewing him at his office, I asked the minister to give a detailed description of the women he thought I was looking for. The pastor replied, "Why, you know, women who are poor and stupid enough to get involved with abusive men. Women in this congregation and community are far too smart for that."

Domestic violence is found only in urban areas.
"Call folks in St. Louis, Chicago, and Kansas City; there's tons of vic-tims in those places," a minister serving a parish in rural Missouri told me. He explained why he thought no abused women live in his small community. "Everybody here knows everything about every-one else," he chuckled. "It would be virtually impossible for a hus-band to be abusing his wife without the entire community hearing about it and confronting the guy about his ugly behavior."

Many clergy members in rural areas whom I approached for an interview declined. Like the minister in Missouri, they insisted that domestic violence is only a "big city problem." My citation of national statistics indicating that one of every three or four American women will be abused in their lifetimes by an intimate or former intimate male partner did nothing to change the thinking of these pastors. "Abused women in this community?" a minister in rural central Wisconsin asked rhetorically. "I suspect domestic violence is prevalent in the Twin Cities [Minneapolis and St. Paul, Minnesota], but definitely not here."

People in rural communities who are involved in the domestic violence movement offered a different perspective. "Thinking that domestic violence occurs only in urban areas is a major fallacy," said Father Michael McDermott, a Catholic priest who pastors Saints Peter and Paul Church in St. Paul, Nebraska, a town of approxi-mately two thousand. "What happens in rural communities such as ours is that people become stagnant. There's a lot of isolation, poor interpersonal development, and a warped sense of learned behav-ior—all of these help to breed domestic violence." Father McDermott explained that many of the victimized women in his community grew up watching their own mothers being emotionally and verbally abused by their fathers. "These women therefore think that the emotional and verbal abuse they receive from their own husbands is normal behavior in marriage. My first task is often to help victims define what domestic violence really is."

John Tschudy has pastored small country churches for a number of years. "I specialize in rural ministry," Tschudy said. "Domestic abuse is as prevalent in rural America as anywhere else. It may be even more prevalent because in a lot of cases people are dealing with isolation." Tschudy discussed the farm crisis in the 1980s. "I was serving in Iowa at the time," he recalled. "There was a tremendous increase in domestic abuse because of the pressure of losing the farm and losing one's lifestyle."

Molly Pandorf, a Christian and licensed clinical social worker, has spent much of her professional career counseling victims of domestic violence in Custer County, Nebraska. A Nebraska native herself, Pandorf addressed some of the myths associated with abused women in her area. "Some people have the idea that because we live in a land of rolling hills and acres upon acres of beautiful farms, we don't have a problem with domestic violence like people do in urban areas," Pandorf stated. "But, per capita, the abuse of women by their husbands in our rural communities is just as prevalent as in any large U.S. city. Out here women and men present an outer image of being self-reliant, strong, and tough. We call this 'rugged individualism.' This makes it much harder for a victim to say, 'I need help.'"

Pandorf also discussed the myth that rural communities are close-knit and supportive. "At times people are very supportive of each other," she admitted. "But, at other times, gossiping takes precedence over caring." As in urban areas, Pandorf said, abused women in rural communities suffer the additional agony of being blamed for their own victimization. "If a wife has a drinking problem, she is told this is the reason her husband abuses her. If she decides to leave the marriage, people judge her all the more. 'How can you take your children away from their father and uproot them from their school?' victims are asked. If an abused wife decides to stay in her marriage—whether out of fear of repercussion from her husband, fear of isolation, fear of not being able to find a job, or for any of a number of other reasons, then the victim is told she must like being abused. It's often a no-win situation for battered women living in rural communities."

Father Bob Rooney also lives in Custer County. He has been a Catholic priest for more than thirty-five years, always in rural parishes. Currently, Rooney pastors St. Joseph's Church in Broken Bow, a community of four thousand residents. "Rural folks face the same problems as people living in urban areas," the priest insisted. "Out here we have alcoholism, personality disorders, domestic violence, etc. There are men in our small community who attempt to get their way by asserting power and control over their wives. The 'rugged individualism' image from the Wild West days is still practiced in this part of Nebraska by many men. And, I think, the image contributes to the ways in which some of these men mistreat their wives."

Myth #4: Victims can stop the battering by changing their behavior. This will save their marriages and families.

These are actually two myths. I've joined them because the clergy members I interviewed treated the concepts as one theme. Both myths carry with them the idea that a wife has the power to control her husband's abusive actions by first changing her own behavior. If the abuse doesn't stop, then the wife is to blame. If the violence ceases, the marriage and family are "saved." Either way, the husband is relieved from responsibility in the matter. The propagation of these myths by clergy members and other Christians have caused victims to suffer added pain, sometimes even death. Let us separate the two concepts in order to illustrate better the dangerous aspects of each.

Victims can stop the battering by changing their behavior.
As we will discuss in chapter 4, men who batter their wives and girlfriends have a number of psychosocial problems. Clergypeople need to understand that none of these problems have anything to do with the behavior of wives or girlfriends. "[B]attering cannot be changed through actions on the part of the victim," write Jacobson and Gottman in *When Men Batter Women.* "Battering has little to do with what the women do or don't do, what they say or don't say. It is the batterer's responsibility—and his alone—to stop being abusive. We collected and analyzed data on violent incidents as they unfolded at home, and examined sequences of actions that led up to

the violence. We discovered that there were no triggers of the violence on the part of the men, nor were there any switches available for turning it off once it got started."[10]

Despite the findings of these two scholars and similar conclusions by other experts in the field, countless numbers of clergy tell battered women that if they would just change their behavior, their husbands' or boyfriends' abuse would stop. Most of the fifty-two survivors I interviewed received this advice from at least one clergyperson. Mary, a survivor whose story is told in detail in the next chapter, sought help from her pastor and his wife after she could no longer endure the ongoing physical, psychological, and sexual torture perpetrated by Edward, her husband, who was an associate pastor at the church. Instead of giving Mary supportive pastoral care, however, the minister and his wife instructed Mary to take a close look at her own behavior. The couple asked Mary how much she was praying, how much time she spent reading the Word, and whether she had any unconfessed sins. Mary was shocked by their questions. "I remember wondering what the questions had to do with how Edward was treating me," she said. "I got the message from my pastor and his wife that I wasn't being spiritual enough, or that I was a sinner because I wasn't reading the Word enough."

By changing their behavior, victims can save their marriages and families.
I will address this misconception frequently throughout the book. Saving the marriage and family at all costs seemed to be the top priority for a number of clergypeople I interviewed, especially men. Intentionally or not, the spiritual leader who embraces this concept implies that the sanctity of marriage is more important than the safety of women and children. This is wrong. "I think the religious community has stressed the sanctity of marriage and the importance of that bond, without any equivocation about the presence of violence," said Rev. Dr. Anne Marie Hunter, an ordained United Methodist minister. She is the founder and executive director of Boston Justice Ministries, which works across denominational and faith lines to inform the religious community about domestic violence. Hunter discussed why victims

might be reluctant to tell their stories to clergy members who are proponents of the "save the marriage and family at all costs" model. "We are seen as a community that would oppose anyone leaving a marriage, even if the husband is violent," Hunter asserted. "As a result of that understanding within the community, often victims are reluctant to go to their pastor or their priest because, after all, we are the people who are talking to them about the sanctity of marriage. So victims may not disclose to us."

Several aspects of this myth concern me. First, instructing women to change their behavior in order to save their marriage and family implies that there is something wrong with the women. This puts the onus of responsibility not where it belongs—with offenders—but on victims. Why are so many clergy bent on blaming women for the acts men perpetrate against them? Second, this myth illustrates the aforementioned issue of placing the sanctity of marriage ahead of the safety of women and children. Not one minister I spoke with would admit to doing this. But when we use phrases like "save the marriage at all costs" we are in fact saying that the bond of marriage is more important than the safety of battered women.

The third reason this myth concerns me is because it's a non sequitur. As we discussed in the preceding section, abusers—and abusers alone—are responsible for changing their harmful behavior. The decision to victimize the women they claim to love is based on their need for power and control. Domestic violence is not caused by, nor can it be corrected by, victims. Finally, I am concerned about the myth that a woman can save a marriage or family by changing her own behavior, because the entire concept is out of order! What are clergy members who believe in and encourage the propagation of this myth really telling abused women? Are they actually advising victims that no matter what their husbands do to them—physically, psychologically, and sexually—victims must remain with these men? Do the ministers truly mean that even if husbands force their wives into performing cruel, degrading, and vile acts, the victims need to stay in the relationship, and change *their* behavior, and then the marriage and family will be "saved"? Would these ministers give the same advice to their own daughters if they were in this situation?

How Clergy Can Effectively Care for Victims of Domestic Violence

Clergy members are in a unique position to help care for victims of domestic violence. We can support these hurting women as they struggle with the many spiritual questions and concerns that result from being violated. "I was a good Christian woman, so I couldn't understand why the abuse was happening to me," said Pamela, a survivor and the daughter of a Lutheran pastor. In the next chapter, we will read about several episodes of the physical, psychological, and sexual battering she suffered from her husband during their nine-year marriage. The abuse caused Pamela to wonder about her spirituality. "I do remember thinking that maybe I was being punished for some unknown sin," she said. "I felt forsaken, not at all thought about by God." Loving and sensitive pastoral care to survivors like Pamela can make a tremendous difference as they face the long and difficult process of healing and regaining trust in themselves and others. Here are some suggestions about caring for victims:

(1) *Listen to and believe victims' stories.* It takes a lot of courage and trust for a victim of domestic violence to share her story with anyone. Her fear of not being believed or of being blamed for the abuse can be overwhelming. (Unfortunately, as we will see throughout this book and especially in the next chapter, they have reason to fear this.) If we appear uninterested in or unbelieving of a survivor's story, she may feel even more fearful, isolated, and violated.[11] When a pastor believes a victim's stories she will feel reassured. Often the victim will blame herself for the abuse, saying the abuse would not be occurring if she were a better Christian, wife, mother, sexual partner, and so forth. That belief is enforced by the perpetrator and, at times, by other people as well. Pastors can say, "You are not the cause of the abuse that's happening to you," and "Your husband's actions are in clear violation of how the Scripture instructs a man to treat his wife. His behavior is sinful and in no way condoned by God."[12]

(2) *Put the safety of victims first.* Many of the clergy members I interviewed told me that "saving" the marriage of a Christian couple

was their top priority. In addition, as we'll see throughout the book, ministers frequently tell Christian wives that they are responsible for the preservation of their marriages and families. This is poor and inappropriate advice. The paramount goal of any domestic violence intervention must always be to ensure the safety of a victimized woman and her children. Nancy Nason-Clark writes in *The Battered Wife*, "The number-one priority in any response to violence against women must be to ensure the physical and emotional safety of the victimized family member. This is the core premise on which the transition house movement has been built. Women victims (and their dependent children) need a place of refuge where they can flee when the circumstances in their home jeopardize their mental or physical health. Clergy and lay religious alike need to be aware of the danger a violent home presents to a woman victim, and they must strive to provide her options that ensure her safety."[13]

(3) *Practice a team approach.* To make the safety of a battered woman and her children the top priority in any domestic violence intervention, clergy and other pastoral ministers must be willing to practice a team approach. Proper training can make us vital members of this team of professionals offering sanctuary to victims. I stress the importance of the team approach, because several of the clergy members I interviewed resisted the idea of collaborating with professionals from the community at large. This worries me.

Even with proper domestic violence education and training, which many ministers do not have, ministers (or those in any other discipline) would still be taking a risk to act as lone rangers when it comes to caring for battered women. Victims need not only spiritual support, but also the emotional, financial, legal, physical, and psychological care of individuals with a wide range of expertise. Sometimes, the immediate needs are paramount: gas for a car, child and medical care, food and housing, etc. Therefore, it is critical for ministers to encourage victims to seek not only our guidance, but also support from other resources. Support groups, shelters for abused women and their dependent children, advocacy workers, attorneys, and clinically trained professionals can offer comfort, knowledge, and safety. A concerted effort by all members of the team will help victims break the isolation and provide them with options for achieving safety in their lives.

(4) *Help victims establish a safety plan.* One specific way a pastor can help a victim of abuse is to help her establish a safety plan that can be implemented quickly should her husband's abuse continue or escalate. Include in this plan a safety kit, kept in a place where the perpetrator will not discover it, that contains items such as cash, a change of clothing, toiletries, an extra photo identification card, and a list of phone numbers of counselors, friends, pastors, and shelters.[14]

Once again, it is crucial that clergypeople work in collaboration with professionals from the community at large. Neil Jacobson and John Gottman stress the importance of this team approach: "Safety planning requires knowledge of the resources, the agencies, and the legal options that exist in the community, which collectively function to provide for safety. The plan usually includes specific strategies for mobilizing whatever informal sources of support exist in [the victim's] life, including but not necessarily limited to friends, family members, physicians, and spiritual mentors, as well as the more formal sources of support that we have already mentioned: shelters, agencies for battered women, housing placement, ways of getting food stamps, and other necessities in the event that they become necessary after [victims] leave the relationship."[15]

(5) *Seek education and training.* Clergy members cannot provide effective and practical spiritual care to victims without obtaining good domestic violence education and training. Supporting battered women is a complicated matter and, even with education and training, ministers must never attempt to be the sole caregivers of victims. Education and training will help us to gain a working knowledge of the complex nature of violence perpetrated against women by an intimate male partner. "The abuse starts very slowly, often with verbal putdowns, and then continues with maybe mild physical pushing and shoving," explains Dr. Lenore Walker, a psychologist and noted pioneer in domestic violence. "The battering is in a cycle, which means there are also positive things that are happening in the relationship. And, in the beginning, the positive is much greater than the negative. So women say to themselves, 'Well, if only I could find a way to make him happier the abuse would stop.'"

Dr. Walker says one of the important aspects of domestic violence education for clergy is that it will reduce our tendency to make women responsible for keeping the family together and safe. "A battered woman doesn't believe it's her fault that her husband is violent," the psychologist said. "But she believes it's her fault for not making the world a better place for him so he doesn't lose control and use violence. That's part of the socialization put on women by clergy, churches, and by religions in general—it's the women's role and responsibility to keep the home environment safe and together. These messages leave women feeling confused and also open to more abuse from their husbands."

Lenore Walker is most famous for her Cycle of Violence Theory. Two-thirds of the four hundred people she studied in the 1970s and 1980s showed evidence of this cycle. The three distinct phases associated with a recurring battering cycle are: (1) tension-building, (2) the acute battering incident, and (3) loving-contrition.[16] Pastoral ministers must gain at least a basic understanding of each phase in order to care effectively for victims.

During the tension-building phase, there is a gradual escalation of tension displayed by discrete acts causing increased friction, such as name-calling, other mean intentional behaviors, and/or physical abuse. The batterer expresses dissatisfaction and hostility, but not in an extreme or maximally explosive form. The woman attempts to placate the batterer, doing what she thinks might please him, calm him down or at least what will not further aggravate him. Phase two, the acute battering incident, is characterized by the uncontrollable discharge of tensions that have built up during phase one. The batterer typically unleashes a barrage of verbal and physical aggression that can leave the woman severely shaken and injured. In the third phase, loving-contrition, the batterer may apologize profusely, try to assist his victim, show kindness and remorse, and shower her with gifts and/or promises. The batterer himself may believe at this point that he will never allow himself to be violent again. The woman wants to believe the batterer and, early in the relationship at least, may renew her hope in his ability to change.[17]

"What I found originally was that there was a three-phase cycle," Walker explained to me. "All the research still supports the three-phase cycle. But the differences that we've learned along the way have been that the loving-contrition or third phase changes. It changes, sometimes over time, and sometimes the whole pattern of the cycle changes even though it's still there. So you don't always see it right away. You have to look very carefully. If you just took a slice of the relationship at any one particular time you might not see it."

It is the third phase of the cycle that leaves untrained clergy members especially vulnerable to deception. As was just discussed, after an abusive episode a batterer will often experience remorse. He may apologize to his victim, seek both her and God's forgiveness, and might even proclaim a total and quick spiritual transformation. Ministers can also be deceived by the behavior of victims if we encounter them during this phase. "The period of loving-contrition reminds the women of the courtship period when the man was Mr. Wonderful," Lenore Walker explained. "It gives her the hope that he will remain that way if only the other two parts would stop. These first two phases, a victim hopes, will eventually become appendages that will drop off and she'll be left with this wonderful person that she fell in love with." It should be noted that this "loving-contrition" is another form of control, and an extension of the manipulation that is already at work in the relationship.

Without proper education and training, and a collaborative spirit, clergy members who encounter a victim and/or her perpetrator during phase three of the cycle could easily be fooled. We could believe that the violence has stopped for good, that the couple are living in a state of permanent bliss, and believe that the marriage and family have been "saved." There is no substitute for ministers seeking the proper education and training we need—and for our willingness to share our expertise in conjunction with the expertise of professionals also working within our communities. If we refuse to take these vital steps, then victims will continue to miss out on the spiritual aspects of care that they both need and deserve.

Conclusion

Who will provide effective spiritual care to domestic violence victims if clergy and other pastoral workers do not? Is it right for us to leave abused women and their children to the mercy of husbands and boyfriends who beat, degrade, rape, or torture them? Can we continue to shirk our responsibilities as spiritual leaders by pledging allegiance to myths that, at best, keep women oppressed and battered—and have sometimes even caused their deaths?

There are battered women worshiping in our congregations. No church is "abuse free," given that one of every three or four American women is abused by an intimate or former intimate partner. Christian survivors need much more than faith, prayer, a positive attitude, and God to be freed from domestic violence. They also need us to stop blaming them for the abuse perpetrated upon them by their husbands and boyfriends, quit telling them that if they'd only change their behavior then marriages and families would be saved, and give them genuine love and support. They also need clergypeople to realize that victims are everywhere, not just in certain cultures, races, or socioeconomic groups, nor only in urban areas.

Who will provide effective spiritual care to victims? It will certainly not be clergy unless we make the long overdue commitment to seek the necessary domestic violence education and training, to work in collaboration with caregivers from other professional disciplines within our communities to ensure the safety of battered women and children, and to believe that domestic violence is not a myth, but a tragic fact of life.

Questions for Discussion

1. Discuss the four myths cited in this chapter. Do you believe in any of these myths? If yes, which ones? Discuss how such misconceptions can be harmful to survivors.

2. List and discuss the three factors that contribute to the belief of many clergy members that there are no abused women in their

congregations. Do you resonate with any of these factors? If yes, tell which ones and how.

3. Have you ever used any of the platitudes listed under myth #2? What influenced your decision to do so? Discuss why trite phrases can bring additional harm to victims.

4. Which is more sacred to you: keeping a marriage together or maintaining the safety of women and children? What do you think clergy members are attempting to communicate to a victim when they tell her to change her behavior in order to "save" her marriage and family? Would you discourage an abused woman from seeking a divorce? If you answer yes, tell why.

5. Are there abused women worshiping in your congregation and living in your community? If you answer no, tell why you think the abuse has passed over your area. If you answer yes, how are you caring for victims and ensuring their safety? Are you working in collaboration with professionals from other disciplines in your community? If yes, how so? If no, why not?

6. Who will provide effective spiritual care to victims if clergy and other pastoral workers do not?

Chapter 3. Survivors Speak Out

Reflections

When I went through some domestic violence training, it all came back to me. I hadn't been in an abusive relationship for a long period of time like some women, but even a couple of years is enough time to do an incredible amount of damage to your spirit. I was taught by other victims that the black and blue marks will go away, and bones will heal. But it's your inner self, your spirit, that takes so long to heal. And, sometimes, you can never heal; you just learn to live with the brokenness.

—Rev. Joan Ishibashi, Minister in the United Church of Christ and Associate Conference Minister for Administration and Resources, Honolulu, Hawaii

There are some striking similarities and some vast differences in the stories told by the fifty-two survivors of domestic violence who allowed me to interview them for this book. (I also interviewed the twenty-two-year-old daughter of one of the victims. As a child she witnessed her father repeatedly abuse her mother and was herself abused by him. And I spoke with a man whose twenty-four-year-old daughter was murdered by an ex-boyfriend.)

All of the women were Christians who were attending conservative, fundamental, moderate, or liberal Catholic or Protestant faith groups at the time they were being abused and battered by their husbands or boyfriends. The perpetrators attended church as well and, according to the victims, they also identified themselves as Christians. (Three of the abusers were parish pastors.) The majority of the victims, when they eventually disclosed the abuse to their ministers, sensed that the pastors did not believe them. Most often the survivors talked about how they felt outright blamed by clergy and other churchgoers for their own victimization. The women I interviewed are African American, Caucasian, Chinese, Filipina, Hispanic, Japanese, Korean, Native Hawaiian, Native American, and Samoan. They are poor, middle class, and rich; some were unemployed and others worked as accountants, administrative assistants, attorneys, homemakers, nurses, physicians, psychologists, social workers, university professors, or ministers. Their ages range from twenty-six to seventy-two.

There is another striking detail about the survivors: although most of them no longer live with their abusers, the vast majority said they feel neither free nor safe from their perpetrators. (Even the women whose abusers have died stated that they still often feel imprisoned by memories of being violated.) This point was emphasized by the fact that nearly all of the victims whose former batterers are still alive currently live an underground existence: their locations and phone numbers are known to virtually no one, save for a few very close intimates. Some of the women have even had to change their names and are now totally cut off from family and friends. The reason for all of this secretiveness was clearly stated: most of the women were told by their perpetrators that one day they'd locate and kill them.

Nevertheless, even with the constant threat of danger, the women said they were eager to share their stories with us. They expressed hope that this would help clergy become better informed about the many complexities associated with domestic violence. All of the stories are true. In every instance, I've recorded verbatim what survivors told me that clergypeople said and did after they learned about the women's abuse. Also, I've recounted word for word the emotional and spiritual repercussions survivors said they felt from being abused and from their pastors' unhelpful responses. In this section, all the names of victims, pastors, and perpetrators have been changed, and certain aspects of the women's stories have been altered to protect their anonymity and safety.

Mary's Story

"I used to think that the physical scars were the worst, but worse still is that my soul was raped."

Mary was raised in an Episcopal congregation. In high school she became a born-again Christian. "Church and God were my life," Mary confessed. "I loved to attend worship, and the pastors and members of the congregation were all like family to me." Mary loved one person above all others: a young Japanese American man named Edward. The two of them dated for a year before deciding to marry. "We were both very athletic people, so we played a lot," Mary reflected. "It was a fun period of time. Edward was one of the associate pastors and we both taught Sunday school classes. He was a fun guy who'd drive across town to save a dog. He was wonderful around kids, very playful and well liked."

Edward was also a wife abuser. Shortly after he and Mary were married, he began to inflict physical, psychological, and sexual torture on his new bride. Mary said that Edward told her that she had to do whatever he instructed, without argument or talking back. The Bible demanded this type of gracious submission from Christian wives, Edward insisted. "I now see that my husband twisted Scripture to justify his twisted ideas," Mary stated. "However, at the time, I didn't know anything other than I loved Edward and, as a Christian wife, I wanted to please my husband. So from that point on I put up with everything he said and did. Only now am I starting to remember all the ways he violated me, including raping me everyday."

Forcing Mary to watch pornography and then to repeat what was played out on the screen, Edward performed such acts on his wife as ramming blunt objects up her anus and vagina. While driving down the freeway, he'd often pull over and force her to perform oral sex on him. If Mary resisted, Edward would beat her.

Things worsened after the couple's twin daughters were born. "I'd be breast-feeding our daughters when, all of a sudden, Edward would begin kicking and yelling at me. That's when I started wearing jeans all the time so no one would see all my bruises. He told me he was jealous of the time I was spending with the babies. This was really confusing to me because I'd quit work to care for our daughters after Edward had insisted that child rearing was my job as a Christian wife. I was becoming more and more frightened because his behavior was now totally unpredictable. He'd blame me if his sandwich was soggy or if our daughters were crying. For no apparent reason, Edward would start cursing at me, saying I was a stupid bitch, a slut, and a whore, then he'd throw pots and pans at my head, or throw food and dishes from the supper table and force me to clean everything up. He took possession of all the money and said this was his right because, as the head of the household, he was in charge of all the finances. I felt trapped. So I turned to the head pastor and his wife for help."

What Mary said she received instead of support was the same three questions asked over and over again. The couple wanted to know how much Mary was praying, how much time she spent reading the Word, and did she have any unconfessed sins. "I remember wondering what the questions had to do with how Edward was treating me," Mary said. "I got the message from my pastor and his wife that I wasn't being spiritual enough, or that I was a sinner because I wasn't reading the Word enough."

Despite the lack of support from the pastor and his wife, Mary remained a faithful member of the church. She said she never considered leaving because "church was our life," and she kept hoping and praying that one of the pastors would confront Edward, minister to minister, about his abusive behavior. "They all knew what my husband was doing," Mary said emphatically. "But, over the years, the pastors began stressing more and more the fact that 'God won't give you any more than you can handle,' and told me I had to remember that 'God calls us to be a living sacrifice.' I really thought this meant I would die at my husband's hands. And I kept wondering why these so-called men of God weren't confronting a fellow pastor about his sins." Mary said that lay members in the church turned their backs as well. One woman friend said that "girls" needed to get back to "family values," and when she told several other women how Edward was abusing not only her but also the children, they replied that this was not possible. Everyone knows Japanese men are passive, they insisted. So Mary had to be mistaken. "Their response made me feel like I was crazy," asserted Mary.

Finally Mary realized she had to take action on her own. She said a light went off in her head after one particular beating that occurred while the couple was vacationing in Europe. "I had begun to notice that Edward's physical abuse was escalating," she explained. "One night in our hotel room in Paris, after accusing me of flirting with a waiter during supper, Edward hit me on the side of my head with his closed fist and I suffered a concussion. He refused to let me go to a hospital, even though I was sick as a dog for three days. Finally I said, 'You really hurt me, Edward.' And, for the first time, he actually admitted he had a problem. 'I know I'm getting more physical with you,' he said. His remorse really shocked me. So a couple of days later when he was in an even better mood, I asked Edward if we could go to counseling after we returned home from vacation. He turned and looked me straight in the eye and said, 'That was just a love tap I gave you the other day. I could really beat the shit out of you.' He then told me that I needed to start doing everything he requested of me or he'd give me more and more beatings like the one I had just received. I was stunned and realized Edward knew exactly what he was doing. I knew then that I had to get out of my marriage or my husband would kill me and the kids."

Mary divorced Edward and is now slowly putting back together the shattered pieces of her life. (Her pastors and other church members told her that God hates divorce and that divorce is a sin. Therefore, they said, it was wrong for her to leave Edward under any circumstance, including abuse.) She continues to receive treatment for post-traumatic stress disorder (PTSD) and also continues to provide support to other victims. Although she feels that she is healing from her twelve years in an abusive marriage, Mary doesn't think she'll ever again feel secure. "I will never feel safe," she declared. "While we were separated Edward threatened to get back at me for leaving him. So I practice safety precautions—I'm careful about where I park, keep an unlisted phone number, and very few people know where I reside. But I will never again feel safe."

Mary says that her greatest loss has been in her spirituality. She eventually left the church she once called her family, and continues to struggle in her relationship with God. (Edward remains one of the pastors at the church. As far as Mary knows he still has not been confronted by any of his ministerial colleagues over his abusive behavior.) "I used to be able to talk with God about anything," she lamented, "but now I can't so there's a big void in my life." She remains angry at the pastors and parishioners who knew about her husband's abuse and did nothing to stop it. "I used to think that the physical scars were the worst, but worse still is that my soul was raped. Each time my husband raped me, and the pastors and church members turned their backs when I went to them for help, a part of my soul was taken away. And I don't know how to get it back. I'm angry at the church, the pastors, and at God, for that matter. I hope that clergy realize how much damage they're causing by not being informed about domestic violence. I wish they could understand that with the right training they'd have a great potential to save battered women from a lot of harm."

Alexis's Story

"Kevin never hit me in the twenty-two years we were married, nor was he ever angry in an identifiable manner. He never raised his voice or called me bad names. The way he abused me was by being manipulative."

There was a dichotomy between female and male roles in the liberal, upper-class, white Presbyterian parish where Alexis was raised. "Our church taught a gospel that was basically sociology with a scriptural text sometimes pinned underneath it very loosely. Back then there was no thought of a woman being ordained. Men were the pastors and elders, women made the sandwiches and took care of babies in the nursery."

Leaving her Colorado home in the late 1960s to attend a prestigious Midwestern university, Alexis said she became even more disenchanted with her church. "It was such a 'be good' religion," she stated. "I was having to live by everyone else's rules. But at the university all of this changed. It was such heady stuff to be a part of the counterculture. I had the attitude that everything that had gone before was either shortsighted or blind. We were the generation who had all the new insight, I told myself. We were going to reshape the world and save us from ourselves. Part of this massive change was to throw out all the religious teaching from the past, which I viewed as just a bunch of empty liturgies and rituals."

By her junior year at the university, however, Alexis was depressed and suicidal. All of the so-called "new insight" of the counterculture had brought her no closer to enlightenment than had the religious teachings from her church back home. "While growing up, I hadn't had the experience of a very present and loving God," Alexis conceded. "And, by the time of my junior year at the university, I'd hit bottom with radical intellectualism as well. I felt destitute, realizing that a life without God was empty." Dead both spiritually and emotionally, Alexis turned to a born-again Christian group where she found comfort and strength. She was especially drawn to Kevin, a young man in the group. "He'd also been raised in a liberal, white church body," recalled Alexis, "and had grown disenchanted with that church's emphasis on social issues rather than matters of the spirit." The couple began dating and they were married shortly after graduating from the university. (Not long after their first date, Kevin said to Alexis, "I think I love you," which Alexis said "stunned" her. He also mentioned that he felt that God was calling him into the Christian ministry. "I really respected the fact that Kevin was almost always at our 7 A.M. prayer meetings," noted Alexis. "He was so disciplined and was someone I thought I could trust. All I wanted to be was a partner in ministry with someone who had a heart strong for God.")

But even before they were married, Alexis said, there were problems in their relationship. "We were being taught good doses of the male headship/female submission theme by a pastor who'd gone to a conservative theological seminary," she recalled. "He'd say, 'The word of God says' this or that, and we accepted it. I remember crying over what I felt was insensitive treatment of me by Kevin. He'd be real neglectful of my feelings and needs. I felt disrespected, but I couldn't put my finger on why. Kevin never hit me in the twenty-two years we were married, nor was he ever angry in an identifiable manner. He never raised his voice or called me bad names. The way he abused me was by being manipulative. He'd withdraw and was very twisting mentally."

According to Alexis, Kevin told her he had a more advanced and sophisticated understanding of right and wrong. He'd watch violent movies with their young children, and would also watch the adult channel late at night. (He kept pornographic material locked in a closet that Alexis discovered later.) "I'd been aware that my husband was gradually withdrawing from our marriage both emotionally and sexually," Alexis confessed. "It was as though he was someone else. He was no longer interested in me sexually and rarely did he even have a conversation with me." When she confronted Kevin about these matters, Alexis said her husband accused her of being judgmental, critical, and cold. "He said he was the pastor, the person who'd gone to seminary, and that my views of the world were simply inferior to his. At the time I didn't see that I was being deceived and manipulated. I was still putting the blame on myself."

Alexis began to see a clearer picture of her husband on the day their six-year-old daughter came to her and said, "Daddy licked my bottom." Confronting Kevin immediately, Alexis said her husband didn't deny the abuse. "He said he was sorry, that this was the only time he'd ever touched our daughter in a sexual way, and that he'd never do it again. Only much later did I discover that the child abuse had begun when our daughter was two or three, and it continued throughout her early teens." When Alexis and Kevin moved to another part of the country, Alexis one day mentioned to a woman at their new church home about her husband's abuse. (Kevin was not the pastor of that parish. By this time he had left the ministry and become a high school teacher.) The woman encouraged Alexis to see the senior pastor of the new congregation. "That man was very astute," Alexis said. "He met with Kevin and me separately. Then one day the minister and two of the church's elders met with me alone. They told me that they felt my children and I were in continued danger for more of Kevin's emotional and sexual abuse. He seemed to have no intention of stopping what he was doing, the church leaders told me. They said Kevin was very intelligent, manipulative, and slippery, and that he was not telling them the truth. 'We're advising you to divorce him,' they concluded. 'It's the only way you and your children will ever be free and safe.'" Alexis found the advice from those church leaders very supportive and freeing. "I would have never ever considered divorce as an option had it not been for those men," she admitted. "Marriage was for life, despite Kevin's ill-treatment of my children and me. Without the pastor and those two elders, I'd still be in that miserable relationship."

Still, Alexis continues to struggle with her spirituality as a result of her marriage to Kevin, and also because of a second marriage to a man who Alexis said abused her both psychologically and physically. "It's been difficult to reach God," she confessed. "Sometimes I'm not sure of the ground I'm on. I feel I've come full circle, that God is back to being a distant figure. But on other days the flame seems to be rekindled. One of the main reasons I've moved to the city where I now reside is because the seminary I want to attend is here. I want to get back into a deeper study of the Scriptures so that I can say, 'I understand the Greek now. This is what God really says about wives and husbands.'"

Marie's Story

"The pastor told me to be my husband's whore."

"I was scared of being alone, scared also that if I left my husband he'd carry out his threat to hurt or kill me." This is why, Marie says, she stayed in an abusive marriage for more than thirty-five years. "I had five children and my husband, Charlie, would tell me that if I ever left him he wouldn't offer child support. He also constantly said no one else would want me. So I stayed even though I'd lost my love and respect for him long ago, and though he'd beaten and raped me throughout most of our marriage. But the last straw came when Charlie started to openly cheat on me. That's when I decided to go to the pastor of my church for help."

Although Marie had obtained a temporary restraining order against Charlie because of his violence toward the children and her, and had told her minister of this order, the pastor still suggested that Marie meet with her husband. "I didn't think it was the best advice," acknowledged Marie. "But I also didn't think that my pastor would put me in danger. So I took my four sons with me to meet Charlie at a nearby park. My daughter refused to go because she feared this was a dangerous meeting. Well, immediately, my husband became verbally abusive, calling me a 'bitch' and a 'good-for-nothing whore.' I now realize that the pastor's advice was not helpful or safe—Charlie could have killed me and the kids. Later I also found out the minister knew that my husband was fooling around with other women at the time he had encouraged me to meet with Charlie."

Despite having the knowledge of both Charlie's marital infidelity and his history of wife abuse, the pastor continued to encourage Marie to stay in her marriage. She couldn't raise five children on her own, the minister insisted, and, besides, the kids needed a father. "Both the senior and associate pastors knew Charlie was abusing me," declared Marie. "They even witnessed some of his verbal abuse. But they did absolutely nothing to support me or to confront my husband. In fact, there was one time when the senior pastor saw Charlie punch our daughter in the face at a church picnic, and the pastor turned and walked the other way."

According to Marie, it was this same pastor that gave her the most degrading advice. He told her she should have sex with Charlie whenever her husband demanded. "The minister advised me to 'put on the heart of Esther' to win my husband back," Marie related. "When I asked him to explain what that meant, the pastor told me to be my husband's whore. Previously, rape had been a major part of our sexual relations. So for the pastor to tell me to whore myself made me feel like the scum of the earth." Marie concluded with a strong warning to victims of domestic violence: "If pastors seem to be thinking only about saving a marriage, as was the case with my pastors, then stay away from those pastors at all costs."

Kelly's Story *(Marie's twenty-two-year-old daughter)*

"I was raised in the church and taught that God is always with us and all knowing. When we pray God hears us, was the message pastors pounded into my head. After living in an abusive home for so long, and after seeing and feeling my father's brutality, I began to feel that God was somebody who had something else to do, that he was not concerned about my life."

"I grew up believing that abuse was normal," reflects Kelly. "If I'd mouth off or the house wasn't clean or dinner wasn't on the table when my dad came home, then I deserved to be beaten. It wasn't normal, I thought, that most of my friends weren't experiencing abuse in their homes. I witnessed my dad totally abuse my mom. He'd call her 'stupid,' 'whore,' and other nasty names. And I remember hearing and seeing a lot of physical abuse. I think I was eighteen before I actually slept by myself. Mom would always come to my room, which was next to hers, and crawl in bed with me after Dad beat her. She knew she was pretty safe while lying next to me. There were nights, however, that Dad would come into my room and start to beat me as well. And, when I was three, he also began sexually abusing me. It angers and sickens me that a father would treat his daughter this way."

Kelly has had a very difficult time dealing with the incongruent aspects of her home and church life. "My father was the men's ministry president and in charge of church administration," Kelly said. "Yet, look at how he treated his family. What angers me most is that the pastors and everyone else in the church knew what Dad was doing, but they did nothing to stop him.

"Everyone was praising and worshiping God, and they kept saying my mom, brothers, and I were making all these horrible stories up to make Dad look like a bad guy. In actuality, he is a bad guy."

Debra's Story

"My Christian friends, so-called Christian friends, were saying to me, 'You're a Christian wife, Debra. Maybe if you stay in your marriage you can lead William to the Lord.' I really struggled with their advice. Perhaps I could have been influential in bringing my husband to Christ. Yet, I had enough insight to know that if I didn't get out of the marriage I was going to die. But nobody, not the ministers nor my friends, was giving me permission to get out. No one ever called my husband on his inappropriate behavior. They simply kept talking about my responsibilities as a Christian wife."

The second of six daughters, Debra was raised in a conservative home and church. "My parents were religious," acknowledged Debra, "but I still wonder if they were actually Christians. Their whole emphasis was on telling us girls to be 'good.' If we weren't good then God would punish us, they'd always say. One of their favorite scriptural passages was 'You reap what you sow.' Our church also had very legalistic views on right and wrong. Anybody who functioned outside of what was taught by the ministers was forced to stand before the entire congregation and publicly confess their sins. This tactic built up so much fear that everyone worked hard at doing the right thing, at being good. Otherwise God, who was portrayed as an angry and scary father figure, would punish us."

Debra met William, her future husband, while the messages from her childhood regarding good and evil were still festering. They'd gone to the same rural elementary school but didn't formally meet until both were attending the same university. Debra was drawn immediately to William's quick wit. "We were both Christians so it seemed as though we never ran out of things to discuss," she remembered. They began dating and were married three years later. Debra went on to earn her master's degree in forestry, while William earned a Ph.D. in philosophy.

According to Debra, William's abuse began a week into their marriage. She had declined for the first time her husband's offer to have sex. He became enraged. "William bolted out of our bed and went straight to the dining room where I kept the china and crystal my grandmother had willed to me," Debra recalled. "He started breaking plates and glasses—and he did not stop until every piece of china and crystal was shattered. I never refused to have sex with my husband again." A few days later William told Debra that he thought the marriage was a mistake. "I was crushed," Debra declared. "I'd worked so hard at trying to please my husband's every desire but, when he said we'd made a mistake getting married, I somehow felt that I had failed. If I could just be a better wife, I told myself, then William would want to stay in the marriage."

The couple began attending a large, conservative parish. Periodically, the men in the church would get together for a time of prayer. As a result of these gatherings, William started telling Debra she had to submit totally to him. This was what the Bible instructed Christian wives to do, William insisted. "I told my husband I wasn't going to submit because it seemed like the perfect set up for a wife to be abused," asserted Debra. "But later I felt guilty for stating my opinion so strongly and, gradually, I gave in." William's idea of wifely submission centered around sexually abusive behavior. He began bringing pornographic videos home, demanding that Debra watch the tapes with him. William told his wife that the videos would "enhance the sexual aspects" of their relationship. "The tapes depicted women either being physically abused or having to perform some degrading act on a man," Debra remembered. "William wanted to replicate these scenes during our lovemaking. I never refused the sex, but there were some things I told William I wouldn't do. He'd get really angry and call me a 'frigid bitch,' 'dumb cunt,' and an 'asshole.' He even told a Christian counselor that we didn't have the sexual intimacy that he wanted in a marriage. What William was asking of me didn't feel like intimacy or love. It was not something I expected or wanted in a marriage, especially a marriage between two Christian people. Still, I believed there was something wrong with me and not my husband."

Debra finally turned for help to the people at the church. She was disheartened by the responses she received. "My Christian friends, so-called Christian friends, were saying to me, 'You're a Christian wife, Debra. Maybe if you stay in your marriage you can lead William to the Lord.' I really struggled with their advice. Perhaps I could have been influential in bringing my husband to Christ. Yet, I had enough insight to know that if I didn't get out of the marriage I was going to die. But nobody, not the ministers nor my friends, was giving me permission to get out. No one ever called my husband on his inappropriate behavior. They simply kept talking about my responsibilities as a Christian wife."

Ten years after the relationship ended, Debra is beginning to see matters in a more accurate light. (William left Debra to marry another woman. Although it was clear even during the marriage that he had been unfaithful as well as abusive, several ministers and Christian friends told Debra that she would have either to take William back if he decided to return to her or remain single for the rest of her life.) "I now know I didn't deserve William's abuse," Debra insists. "I'm beginning to realize how manipulative he was. I reread my diary recently and can now see that William was a master at blaming me for his issues."

Debra is angry at the ministers who provided inaccurate biblical information to her. "If pastors are going to open their mouths about submission," she maintained, "then they sure as hell better be teaching that a husband is to love his wife as Christ loves the church. If ministers are not teaching a husband's responsibilities in a marriage, then they aren't fulfilling their commitment to the Lord. They're preaching only half-truths." She describes her current relationship with God as murky. "I try so hard to think about the love of God, and I've put a lot of effort into learning to know God better. Still, I struggle with the idea of God as a male and all the abuse males perpetrate in the world. So I'm learning to know God as a whole different person. I'm beginning to think of being led by a God of love, instead of a God tied up in all of this submissive and abusive crap."

Esperanza's Story

> "I told the priest about my husband's infidelity, and also about his verbal, physical, and economic abuse. I wanted a divorce, I said. But the priest replied, 'When you got married, you vowed to stay married for life.' I told him that my husband broke the vows of our marriage covenant when he

chose to abuse me, then I asked the priest for absolution. But the priest responded, 'Sorry, I can't do that, a vow is a vow. You vowed to stay married for life. Leave the confessional now.' I walked out of the booth in a state of shock."

Esperanza had reached the lowest point of her life, emotionally and spiritually. Having lived for almost fifteen years with Hector, a man who had constantly abused her physically, psychologically, and verbally, she realized that if she didn't get a divorce, she'd end up in prison for murdering him. "I was sick and tired of being battered by Hector," confessed Esperanza, who now facilitates groups for abused and battered women, and separate groups for perpetrators of domestic violence. "He'd taken away my dignity, pride, self-esteem, and all my money. I was getting kicked out of my apartment after losing a very good paying job as a hairdresser. I had no support system and had no idea there was such a thing as a shelter for battered women. I felt like nothing, so I knew I had to leave or I was going to kill my husband."

In the midst of her despair, Esperanza turned to her priest for help. She'd been a devout Catholic her entire life and, realizing the church's stand against murder, she decided to seek a divorce rather than to commit a crime. "I went to my priest for help, but instead he asked me to leave the confessional," Esperanza lamented. "I told the priest about my husband's infidelity, and also about his verbal, physical, and economic abuse. I wanted a divorce, I said. But the priest replied, 'When you got married, you vowed to stay married for life.' I told him that my husband broke the vows of our marriage covenant when he chose to abuse me, then I asked the priest for absolution. But the priest responded, 'Sorry, I can't do that, a vow is a vow. You vowed to stay married for life. Leave the confessional now.' I walked out of the booth in a state of shock. So there I was with no money, no job, and being abused in all kinds of ways by my husband. And the biggest support systems I'd known my entire life—God, Christ, the Catholic Church—had turned their backs on me. I had nothing and no one. As a result of that priest, I stayed away from church for more than twenty years."

Pamela's Story

"I was a good Christian woman, so I couldn't understand why the abuse was happening to me. I do remember thinking that maybe I was being punished for some unknown sin. I felt forsaken, not at all thought about by God."

For nine years Pamela, the daughter of a Lutheran minister, lived in a type of hell. Her husband, Kai, controlled her every move. "After a month of marital bliss life turned into a nightmare," says Pamela. "Kai was not at all the man I thought I had married. Even though he was at work all day, I'd have to leave him a note regarding all my activities: buying gas for the car, visiting my best friend, walking our dog. When I went to the grocery store, I wasn't to even make eye contact with or talk to male clerks. Kai's rationale for all the controlling behavior was that he just didn't trust other men. Yet, he also cut me off from my family. I was rarely allowed to go over to my parents' home—even after I'd given birth to their first grandchild. Ultimately, I could only associate with Kai and his family. I couldn't see anyone I cared about or anyone who cared for me."

Constantly concerned that his wife would meet someone "smarter" than himself, Kai began to verbally ridicule Pamela, telling her she was "too good of a person and too honest," while, at the same time, calling her "bitch," "cunt," and "stupid." Eventually, he began to abuse her both physically and sexually. "I'd come home from work and, immediately, Kai would humiliate me by examining my vaginal area to make sure I hadn't had sex with another man," Pamela stated. "And I'll never forget the first time my husband hit me. As I was walking away from him during one of our many arguments, he slapped me on the back of my head. When I turned to face him, Kai kicked me in the stomach. I was shocked, scared, and felt totally demolished. Later he apologized, and said it would never happen again, so I took him back. But the physical, sexual, and psychological abuse escalated. After I got a restraining order against him, Kai stalked me and kidnapped our daughter. He kept her from me for several days. Another time, he cut the brake lines on my car. When I finally told him I was going to leave the marriage, my husband replied, 'If you do, bitch, I'll kill you.' At the same time he purchased an expensive diamond ring for me and begged my forgiveness. He even said he'd go to counseling if I stayed. I was totally confused. By the time I left Kai I had become nothing more than a robot, just a shell of a person. There was such a void in my spirit. I could get up, get dressed, and feed and clothe my daughter, but I was just a shattered soul. I was a good Christian woman, so I couldn't understand why the abuse was happening to me. I do remember thinking that maybe I was being punished for some unknown sin. I felt forsaken, not at all thought about by God."

Although he never used Scripture to justify his abuse, Kai did prevent Pamela from attending church, calling himself "the king of the castle" and her "Lord." After divorcing her husband, Pamela returned to her religious roots, the Lutheran church. "I went back to church primarily to look for answers as to why I'd been abused by Kai," confessed Pamela. "The pastor at my parish was female and also named Pamela, which made me feel that she had been sent by God. Pastor Pamela was a very lovely woman with a comforting voice. She allowed me to tell my story without interjecting any judgments. I'd never told anyone about what Kai had done to me, not even my family. Life was so painful, and I was spiritually lost. Pastor Pamela gave me plenty of space and time. 'What you've been through has been terribly unfair and wrong,' she said. 'It took a lot of courage and trust for you to share your story with me. I'm here to support you.' Her gentle and nonjudgmental approach was an important first step on my lifelong road to spiritual recovery."

What Survivors Need Clergy to Know

Most of the fifty-two survivors I interviewed were angered, disappointed, and hurt by the ways in which clergypeople responded to their reports of abuse. The survivors believe that ordained ministers do not provide appropriate or consistent care to victims, misinterpret Scripture to support male dominance and female subjugation, blame victims for their abuse, hesitate to confront perpetrators, deny the prevalence of domestic violence within their own congregations, and pressure victims to stay in dangerous marriages. The survivors also said that clergypeople refuse to educate themselves about domestic violence and don't take advantage of the myriad resources available on the subject.

I asked the seven women whose stories appear in the first part of this chapter what they need clergy members to know about domestic violence. Here's what they said:

"Clergy need more education about domestic violence. They have to hear with their hearts, and not just their brains. Clergy need to know that one incident of abuse—physical, psychological, sexual, or verbal—can break the spirit of a victim."

—ESPERANZA

"Clergy must listen to victims with compassion and concern. They need to recognize that victims are broken by their perpetrators. Life is so painful, especially after we begin to talk about the abuse. Clergy really need to care for us and believe our stories."

—PAMELA

"All I ask of pastors is that if they don't know how to deal with abuse in families, then they need to find out how. There are so many resources out now, domestic violence is no longer just a dirty little secret. Pastors need to learn the numbers to shelters by heart. Every church should have a food pantry and money set aside for women trying to escape abusive situations. When we're trying to run away from our batterers, we ain't got no money. The perpetrators have all the money."

—KELLY

"I want clergy to know that domestic violence occurs among couples worshiping in their churches. They may not look for it, and, even when it's right in front of them, clergy might try to deny it. But it's there, nonetheless."

—ALEXIS

"Pastors have a responsibility to learn not only what the Bible is saying, but also what's happening in today's world. As Christians, we may not be of this world, but we are certainly affected by what happens in this world, like domestic violence. Pastors need to realize that domestic violence happens all over the world, including between the people who attend church. Clergy have to open their eyes to this fact."

—MARIE

"Clergy need to tell victims that their male partners shouldn't be saying or doing abusive things to them. If a man crosses the line, either by calling his partner inappropriate names or in what he does physically and sexually, clergy need to have a clear understanding that the behavior is abusive. And when men are abusive in any way to their partners, clergy must confront these men immediately."

—DEBRA

"My belief is that women turn first to ministers and members of the medical profession when they decide to disclose episodes of domestic violence. So clergy need to name the abuse. They need to understand that even if a victim does not have any broken bones or bruises, she still could be experiencing abuse. There is psychological and sexual abuse in so many marriages. Clergy shouldn't ask a victim why she's staying in an abusive marriage. Pastors need to also realize that there are many men sitting in the pews of their churches who go home after the service and abuse their wives."

—MARY

A Father's Story

Hi Dad!!

Surprise! You probably thought I forgot about you. I didn't. I save all my messages I get from people until I have time to respond back.

How is work going? Are you ready for Christmas? I decorated my tree and put up my Christmas village yesterday. You should come and see my decorations. They are pretty, and they make me happy.

So, what is the plan for Christmas Eve? Is that when we're hav-
ing Christmas? I assume it is, but no one has really said anything.
Just let me know. I have the entire day off. I really like e-mail. It is
a great way to communicate. I'll talk to you later.
Love, Rachel 12-15-97

What follows is an account of a father's ongoing grief and suffering resulting from the murder of his daughter by a former boyfriend. All names, places, and events are real. I thank Terry Boer for his willingness to share.

In the early morning hours of Saturday, December 20, 1997, twenty-four-year-old Rachel Leah Boer returned home to her small apartment in Oskaloosa, Iowa. She'd been at a Christmas party sponsored by the company where she worked as the marketing services coordinator. Unbeknownst to Rachel, a man had broken into her apartment while she was at the party and was hiding in the bathroom. The man was no stranger. Darin Burck and Rachel had dated on and off for several years. But in the days leading up to that final Saturday before Christmas, Rachel had told the thirty-one-year-old man that things just weren't working out. Their romance was over for good. So Darin Burck decided to grant Rachel Boer her expressed wish for a permanent ending to their relationship: he shot her to death and then did the same to himself. "When two police officers came to my home and told me Rachel had died, I immediately assumed she'd been in a car wreck," recalled Terry Boer. "Never once did I ever imagine that any of my children would be murdered."

Boer said the initial shock and disbelief he felt over Rachel's death turned quickly to anger. He was furious at Darin Burck, a man he'd never met, for choosing violence rather than seeking healthier ways to deal with his insecurities. "Darin committed a selfish act," Boer declared. "There's nothing that ever could condone what happens in any form of domestic violence. That behavior is always about someone trying to control another person's life." But the grieving father was also angry at Rachel and her friends. "It was like they all agreed to participate in a conspiracy of silence," was Boer's description of the way his daughter and her friends kept Burck's behavior hidden from him. "I found out after Rachel's death that she had talked to other people about her growing uneasiness around Darin. As a matter of fact, three weeks before her murder, Darin had broken a window in Rachel's apartment; and no one told me about it."

Terry Boer doesn't remember much about the first few months after Rachel's death. "Things were like a blur," he said. "My mind didn't want to connect with reality." He does recall, however, two dreams. "I had the first dream about a month after Rachel died," Boer said. "She was angry and suspicious towards me. It ended with her running off. Two months later I had a pleasant dream about her. Rachel came up to me and gave me a big hug. She said, 'Everything is OK,' and then just faded out of the picture. To me that dream was very therapeutic." Still, the grieving father endured a lot of emotional distress. "It was very difficult the first six months, hard on my family and hard on me. It seemed like there were these stages I went through." In addition to shock, disbelief, and anger, Boer faced sadness, depression, recollection, and recrimination in the first half-year after his daughter's death. "For quite a while I'd see Rachel everywhere, especially the places I'd been with her. And I kept recalling things we'd said in the past. I couldn't look at old pictures either, because it just hurt too much. At some point I started blaming myself for Rachel's death. Maybe I could have prevented it from happening. I kept thinking about things that could have been different."

This father is particularly haunted by a conversation he had with his daughter the last time he saw her alive. "Rachel and I talked a little bit about who she was dating and stuff," he remembered. "She told me about her and Darin, and that they were kind of on and off. Well, for some reason I felt very uneasy about what she was telling me, I can't remember why. But something triggered me to ask Rachel if she was safe, if she thought maybe I should talk with him. It seemed from what she was telling me that Darin was pretty controlling. But Rachel said, 'No, no, Dad, Darin wouldn't hurt anybody.'"

A week and a half later, Darin Burck murdered Rachel Boer.

After Rachel's death, well-intentioned people offered Terry Boer advice that he didn't find helpful. "I had people say, 'God works in strange ways. You just don't understand it right now.' And a lot of people told me that Rachel should have quit dating Darin a long time ago. But this statement just took the blame away from the person who killed my daughter." Many other people told Boer that Rachel's death was "God's will." The father said he was especially troubled by this advice. "I don't think it's God's will that anybody dies the way Rachel died," he insisted. "It's certainly not God's will that we control somebody else's life. We have to control our own lives. All of us have free will—if we want to do things, we do them; if we don't, we don't. It isn't God's will that Rachel had a relationship with Darin that ended up with her being murdered by him. God didn't want my daughter to end up that way."

Terry Boer received warm and sensitive spiritual care from the Rev. Dr. Peter Fribley. For eleven years Dr. Fribley pastored the First Presbyterian Church in Oskaloosa, which Boer and his family still attend. Although he moved to Madison, Wisconsin, prior to Rachel's death, the Boer family asked Fribley to officiate at her funeral. "Peter's sermon was very poignant and well delivered," Boer reflected. "Many of the more than four hundred people who attended the service told me how touched they were by his words. He talked about how women need to claim their space, and how men have to not be so controlling. It was very moving." Even during the first few months after his daughter's death, the time he now refers to as "a blur," Terry Boer can recall several ways in which Fribley effectively ministered to him. "Peter was never pushy," he explained. "He'd let me talk if I wanted to talk, and would be with me in silence if I didn't want to talk. This helped me to put Rachel's and my life in some sort of context, to see where our place is in the world." The pastor continues to e-mail Boer, allowing the father to grieve and heal at his own pace. "I told Peter recently that I still don't really know how I'm supposed to grieve," confessed Boer. "I mentioned that maybe a year of sackcloth and ashes would be sufficient. And Peter continues to listen to me without judgment."

Rachel Boer's murder has also changed how her father views his role as a parent. "No longer do I think that I have any control over my children's lives—only influence," he said recently. One of the influences Terry Boer is trying to have on his children is to help them to pay close attention to their own instincts. "From what I've heard since her death, I now think that Rachel knew that Darin wasn't a good person to be around," he stated. "But there were times in her life when she felt that she had to have a boyfriend—maybe to go to this dance or to accompany her on some shopping trip. Rachel always had to have some man with her. She didn't want to be home alone on Saturday nights. I now tell my kids that if they feel like something is not quite right, they need to trust those instincts." Boer offers additional counsel to his younger daughters, now ages four and six. "I'm trying to tell them that they have choices and feelings that are important," he said. "They don't need to have somebody leading them around."

He is troubled about the messages that the media gives girls and women. "I'm trying not to let my daughters watch all of this Walt Disney crap," he explained. "You know: the stories where the prince comes riding up on a white horse. It's the same message that is portrayed on TV in soap operas. We don't even have a TV. We got rid of it over a year ago because of all the negative messages it sends to females, the number one message being that females have to have a boyfriend or husband to be of value in the world. I tell my girls that when they get older they don't have to have a boyfriend or get married. They can make decisions for themselves and do anything they want on their own."

I asked Terry Boer to offer, as both a grieving father and mature Christian, some advice to clergypeople. "Domestic violence is about not talking" to loved ones about one's fears," he replied. "That's why abusers get away with it. The happiest woman in your congregation might be the most abused person at home. I could be wrong, but I think if Rachel had told me, 'Dad, Darin's giving me some trouble, maybe you should talk to him,' I would have gone and talked to him. It might not have helped anything, but it might have made him think. But, like many victims, my daughter was ashamed and afraid so she said nothing to me. And that's the thing clergy need to realize: just because someone isn't saying she's facing a problem doesn't mean that everything is OK."

Questions for Discussion

1. Discuss the insights you gained from reading the stories of survivors of domestic violence. What did you find helpful or troublesome about the way clergypeople responded to these survivors? Why?

2. Name and discuss how you would address the various excuses used by perpetrators to justify their abuse of a wife or girlfriend. What would you say to victims about these justifications? What about the perpetrators?

3. Discuss your thoughts and feelings after reading Terry Boer's story. How would you minister to a parent whose child was murdered by an intimate partner?

4. What approaches will you now take to provide effective and practical spiritual care to victims and their children?

Chapter 4. Once an Abuser, Always an Abuser?

It's a troubling question, and I struggle with it all the time: can abusive men change? And it's always brought home, more than at any other time, after a man's been through treatment and he appears to have done well. He's struggled with issues, seems to have resolved them, and so on. Yet, he abuses his partner again. That's when it becomes the most frustrating to do my work.

—DR. L. KEVIN HAMBERGER, CLINICAL PSYCHOLOGIST, MEDICAL COLLEGE OF WISCONSIN, RACINE FAMILY PRACTICE RESIDENCY PROGRAM, RACINE, WISCONSIN

As demonstrated in the preceding chapter, perpetrators of domestic violence are found not only in the secular world. Some are faithful churchgoers, even pastors. There are men who sit in the pews and stand in the pulpits of our congregations, serve on our church boards and teach in our Sunday school classes, men who proclaim the love of Jesus Christ, who abuse and batter their wives and girlfriends. And if we are to fulfill our roles as spiritual caregivers to all the people in our "flock," ministers will eventually have to confront the abusive behavior of these men. As is the case with victims, however, dealing with abusers is a delicate matter requiring a well thought-out plan and approach. When intervening in domestic abuse situations, pastors need to work with a team of professionals from several other disciplines. They must be well trained in identifying and understanding the complex profile of the abusive man.

Even with spiritual counseling and abuser treatment, can perpetrators of domestic violence change their ways? It's a disturbing question that has gnawed at me since I started work on this project.

The fifty-two survivors I interviewed held little hope that lasting change could occur. After years of living with men who beat, humiliated, raped, and threatened them, men who repeatedly made seemingly sincere promises never to abuse them again and to seek professional help, only to break all their promises, most survivors told me that perpetrators of domestic abuse could never truly change. "My husband changed enough to keep me from filing criminal charges against him for the constant physical beatings he gave me, and to prevent me from threatening his reputation in the community and our church," one victim told me. "After I finally divorced him, I realized he hadn't changed a bit. He was the same physically and sexually abusive bastard I'd married twenty-nine years earlier."

What constitutes abuse in an intimate partnership? Who are the men that violate women they claim to love? Can these men change their harmful behavior? What do clergypeople need to know about perpetrators of domestic violence in order to care for them? Let us begin considering these questions with the true story of a former batterer. His name has been changed and certain aspects of the story have been altered to maintain his anonymity.

Edgar's Story

"I was eighteen when I first hit a woman," Edgar stated matter-of-factly. "I did it just to let her know I was in control, that I was a man." But the sixty-year-old counselor and facilitator of groups for men who abuse and batter their intimate partners now says his violation of women went far beyond physical force. "I also objectified females," admitted Edgar. "I thought I was better than women and told myself that most females were useful only to gratify my sexual needs. So I did a lot of lying and manipulating to get what I wanted from them."

Raised in a home where he and his younger sister were taken to church regularly by their mother and father, Edgar has fond memories of his Christian roots. "The image I still warmly embrace from my childhood is of a loving Jesus who cared personally for me," he acknowledged. "Church was our extended family. There were rules and regulations to follow, but I knew everything would be taken care of. The pastor was a kind man and an authority figure. His word, though maybe not as important as my father's, was to be honored and respected. And if I was doing something I wasn't supposed to, he'd give a certain look that let me know I was in trouble."

Although he described his father as gentle and loving toward his mother ("In the sixty-five years they've been married, I've never seen Pop hit or raise his voice in anger toward Mom"), Edgar disclosed that he and his sister were often the victims of their father's rage. "There's no doubt in my mind, with the current laws in this state and across the country, that what Pop did to me and my sister while we were growing up would now be considered criminal child abuse," Edgar asserted. "He'd beat us with both ends of his belt, with switches and, when I was a teenager, Pop started punching me in the face with his fists. The force of his blows often knocked me down."

Most of the time, Edgar said, he was puzzled as to what he had done to deserve his father's beatings or what he could do to stop them. "My father didn't usually talk much. But while hitting me he'd constantly be yelling at me to stop crying. So I forced myself to be manly, to hold in my tears. However, that didn't work either. I must have come across to my father as being defiant because, when I wouldn't cry, he'd beat me even harder and for a longer period of time. I was totally confused, not knowing what I could do to stop or ease the beatings Pop was giving me."

As he grew older and stronger, Edgar attempted to protect his sister, two years his junior, from having to endure the same punishment he was facing. "My father didn't bloody my sister's nose or blacken her eyes like he'd often do to me," Edgar noted, "but he would punch her in the face with his fists, especially if she came home late from a date. I remember the many times that Mom and I would try to pull Pop off my sister. At other times, I'd step in between my father and sister and, as a result, Pop would beat up both of us."

Edgar was eighteen the last time his father physically abused him. He calls that final episode a battle between an old and a young lion.

"By my late teens, I was bigger and stronger than Pop," Edgar noted. "But he was still in excellent shape. One night he was angry about something I had said or done, I can't remember what. And my father punched me in the face with his fist. Unlike the past, however, this time I just stared at him—I didn't cry, flinch, or fall. I felt really proud of myself for being able to take Pop's best punch without so much as blinking my eyes. I used that moment as a kind of bragging right. It was like I was saying to my father, 'Old man, I can take anything you dish out. You can't hurt me anymore.' And this old lion/young lion image shot into my head. Pop never even attempted to hit me again."

While the wounds from his childhood abuse were still festering deep inside him, eighteen-year-old Edgar began dating several women. "I had a real pimp mentality," he confessed. "I didn't use physical force on most of the women I went with, but I was dishonest." Saying anything to get women to have sex with him, Edgar made promises he had no intentions of keeping. "I told several women that they were my one and only sweetheart, and I constantly insinuated to them that we'd be married after I finished college. I did all of this trust-betraying with no remorse, just to get women in bed. Then, along the way, I met my first wife, Jane."

Intelligent and beautiful, Jane attended the same university as Edgar and, like him, she was majoring in political science. "We were opposites in every way," Edgar reflected with a smile. "Jane was a liberal and an early, outspoken advocate for women's rights. And I was this conservative chauvinist with a crew cut, and a staunch supporter of Richard Nixon in his presidential race against Jack Kennedy. Despite our differences, we fell deeply in love and were married in 1961."

A year later, Jane gave birth to the first of the couple's three sons. After taking a short maternity leave, the young mother planned to return to the university to complete her degree. This did not sit well with her husband. "I had a real cavalier attitude," Edgar admitted. "A mother's place was in the home with her child, I told my wife. When Jane protested, I slapped her hard across the face. She slapped me back and then I started punching her with my fists all over her body. I beat Jane so badly that she was unrecognizable."

Enraged and unrepentant, at the time Edgar blamed his wife for his brutality. "I wanted to show Jane, once and for all, that I was boss," he said. "And I can still remember the phrase I repeated while I was beating her: 'You need to listen to me and start doing every-thing I tell you.' Jane needed to understand that I was the head of our household."

After his rage subsided, Edgar said he began to feel a deep sense of shame. "I was so ashamed of what I'd done that I didn't even want Jane to look at me," he lamented. "I didn't want to be reminded of how I'd disfigured her. Jane didn't press charges. In fact, she didn't even tell the staff at the hospital where she was being treated what had really happened to her. But even though I never placed a violent hand on my wife again, I couldn't stand the fact that I'd brutally attacked the woman I had promised to love and respect when we exchanged wedding vows."

Despite his shame, Edgar didn't seek treatment for his violence or for his control needs. "I didn't have the kind of understanding back then that I now have about abusive men," he explained. "So, while she was still in the hospital recovering, I'd pass little intimate notes to Jane through her girlfriend that said something to the effect that I was really sorry for hurting her. At the same time I made it clear that I thought she was the cause of my violent outburst. If she'd only do what I tell her, I insisted, then I would have no cause to hit her again."

Though Edgar never again physically abused Jane, his emotional and verbal battering never stopped. "I wouldn't relinquish the notion that, as a man, I was smarter than women and entitled to whatever I wanted," he confessed. Jane grew more and more tired of her husband's chauvinism and control and, after eighteen years of marriage, the couple divorced. Refusing to seek treatment, Edgar continued his pattern of abuse in his intimate dealings with other women. "I never hit any of them," he said of his behavior toward women in the early 1980s. "But my patriarchal attitude and betrayal of trust continued. I kept deceiving and using women. Some of them simply wanted to talk politics with me. I could certainly do that for a while, but my primary aim was to get these women into bed."

In 1981 Edgar happened to meet a woman named Ruth whom he had dated a quarter of a century earlier when they attended the same high school. The two middle-aged professionals rekindled their romance and, after learning that Ruth was expecting their child, married in 1982. "The three years Ruth and I dated in high school clearly demonstrate the dichotomy of my life," Edgar explained. "Even in the midst of all the lying and manipulating I was doing back then, there were those young women I neither abused nor misused. We shared a warm and mutually respectful relationship."

But in the early 1980s, Edgar still had not addressed his attitude toward women nor his insecurities. "I thought I had a handle on my past," he declared. "Ruth and I were so deeply in love and happy that I told myself the past was forgotten. Yet, I still hadn't gone through any kind of counseling." Edgar and Ruth remained in a state of bliss throughout Ruth's pregnancy and during the first few months after she gave birth to their daughter. But gradually Edgar started controlling his wife's world.

He demanded that Ruth immediately stop attending a weekly Sunday brunch with her two sisters and their mother, a ritual the four women had established a decade earlier. "I told my wife her place was at home with me and our daughter," Edgar recalled, "and not with a bunch of 'cackling old hens.' This really hurt Ruth because she was very close to her family. But when she started crying, I belittled her. 'What in the hell are you crying about, you stupid woman?' I shouted. 'It's just a dumb ass brunch.'" Edgar said he now realizes he made the decision to have Ruth stop attending the Sunday brunch simply to exercise power over her. "Back then, this kind of twisted demand made me feel better about myself and in control," he said.

While Edgar was on a business trip a few months later, someone phoned Ruth and said that her husband was having an affair with another woman. "The charges were totally bogus," insisted Edgar. "My days of womanizing were over." So was his use of physical force to control women—or so he thought. But when he returned home from the trip and learned that his wife believed the allegations of marital infidelity, Edgar relied on his old ways of dealing with issues.

"We had company in our home at the time, so I suggested to my wife that we go out on the deck to finish our discussion. When we got outside, Ruth told me that I'd better get a lawyer because she had filed for divorce. 'I told you I would never accept your cheating on me,' she said. I was crushed and asked her how could she believe I was unfaithful." As Ruth turned to walk away, Edgar grabbed his wife by her throat, lifted her off the ground, and began slamming her head against the brick wall. "I screamed at Ruth, 'You can't do this to me; I'll kill you before I let you destroy this marriage!' I then released her and she ran back into the house, terrified."

Edgar said he knew exactly what he was attempting to communicate by his show of force. "I wanted to send Ruth my usual controlling and brutalizing message," he said. "I was the man in my house and no woman, especially my wife, was going to question my veracity or faithfulness. Even if I had cheated, it was still my attitude that a wife had no right to question the behavior of her husband."

Nevertheless, Edgar told Ruth that he was wrong for victimizing her. He even promised to seek treatment. "I was sincere about getting help," Edgar remembered, "but I didn't think I really needed it. I was just upset because Ruth didn't believe me. So, in essence, I now see that I was still blaming my wife for my behavior."

Determined to repair their relationship, Edgar stayed in treatment even though he didn't believe he had a problem. "I wasn't working on any issues," he confessed. "I just wanted to appease Ruth so that she wouldn't leave me." Then one day Edgar came home from work and discovered that Ruth had changed all the locks on the doors of their large suburban home. She had also filed criminal charges against him for physically attacking her. "My second wife was extremely astute and safety oriented," Edgar affirmed. "I'd attacked her in July. By the end of August, I could no longer get into my own home and the police were waiting to arrest me on charges of domestic violence. That was the end of my second marriage. Ruth and I never lived together again."

But even though he had been ordered by the court to stay away from Ruth, except to pick up and return their infant daughter during his visitation times, Edgar still sought opportunities to talk with his estranged wife. "I kept hoping and praying that we'd get back together," he admitted. "I desperately needed Ruth to know how sorry I was for hurting her, and that I was now a changed man. I was still in treatment, and had even rededicated my life to God after being away from him since the days of my youth."

Around Christmas that same year, Edgar was certain it was time to talk with Ruth. "I felt that God was telling me to reconcile with my wife," he said. "So one day when I was returning our daughter, I asked Ruth if we could talk for a few minutes." Still angered and frightened by the physical attack he had perpetrated against her, Ruth told Edgar she wanted nothing to do with him. "As far as she was concerned, I was the same vicious man who had threatened to kill her only a few months earlier," Edgar stated. "So she quickly took our daughter out of my arms and began walking back into the house."

Edgar said he then reached out and grabbed Ruth, who slipped while pulling away from him. She hit her face on the concrete and dropped their baby. "Fortunately, our daughter wasn't hurt," he sighed. But Ruth suffered facial bruises from her fall. As a result of this physical altercation, she requested that a permanent restraining order be placed against her husband. Edgar was put on probation and ordered into a batterers' treatment program. "That's when I finally began my lifelong journey toward psychological and spiritual wholeness," confessed Edgar. "Previously, I'd gone into treatment and returned to church to impress Ruth, in the hopes of winning her back. After I committed the second episode of physical violence against her, however, I knew our relationship was over for good. So, I entered treatment this time with the idea that it was somehow going to be for my spiritual and psychological well being."

But soon after beginning his twenty-three-week treatment program, Edgar discovered that achieving his goal of becoming a healthy, nonviolent member of society was easier to wish for than to realize. The six-foot, four-inch man, who normally weighed 230 pounds, shrank quickly to a 160-pound skeleton during the early weeks of treatment. "I didn't want to live," Edgar said definitively. "I was angry at being ordered into treatment by the court and stuck on blaming Ruth for the abuse I perpetrated against her. Yet, I also knew that things weren't right with me. It may sound ridiculous, but I really did love my wife. I now know that you shouldn't violate the people you love, but I did love Ruth, and I didn't want to live without her." Deteriorating emotionally, physically, and spiritually, Edgar spent most of his time in those early group sessions crying. "I'd lost everything: my wife, daughter, even my well-paying job. I was struggling to make ends meet. Still, I kept insisting that I shouldn't even be in treatment. Group was for those men who lacked self-control and were sick, I told myself. Even though I knew I had some problems, I thought I was certainly more healthy than the other men in the program."

During the first eight sessions, Edgar maintained a hostile and superior attitude toward the group's facilitator, the other men in treatment, and God. (At one session he pointed his middle finger skyward and said, "God, this is all I have to say to you.") He gradually began to take a closer look at himself as he started the third month of the program. A key turning point came when one of the other court-ordered participants asked him two simple questions. "Like me, this man had once been married to a beautiful and intelligent woman, they'd had three or four children, and he used to be financially secure," Edgar recalled. "But he abused his family and eventually lost everything. He'd sit quietly every week and listen to me mope about my innocence and brag about how smart I was. Then one day he softly asked, 'Edgar, if you're truly innocent and so brilliant, then why in the hell were you ordered into treatment? And why aren't you at home loving your wife and playing with your little baby?' His questions really challenged me to begin taking ownership for my life. And gradually I stopped being so hostile toward the other members of the group."

Edgar had a difficult time forgiving himself for all the hurt he had caused his two wives and countless other women, and began to experience true remorse as his treatment continued. "Unfortunately, what was sometimes still motivating me was how badly I was hurting—not the hurt I had caused women with my physical, emotional, and verbal abuse," he acknowledged. "But, more and more, I was starting to take total responsibility for my behavior." Edgar also began to experience a real faith renewal. "I'd pointed my middle finger toward heaven and cursed God," he lamented. "This act, and all the womanizing, showed how totally decadent my life was. Still, I had the strong sense that God was willing to forgive me if I'd surrender all of my arrogance and brokenness to him." A woman friend invited Edgar to church and he accepted her offer. "When I went back this time, when I asked Jesus to forgive my many sins, it wasn't some pseudo-act of repentance to try to save my marriage or spare me the humiliation of being ordered into treatment. Instead, I begged for God's forgiveness because I began to truly realize all the hurt I'd caused women with my actions and behavior."

Toward the end of his twenty-three weeks in treatment, Edgar was approached by the group's facilitator. "He introduced me to the coordinator of the program, and told the coordinator that I was a guy who had worked hard on my issues and possessed the skills to become a facilitator myself," Edgar remembered. Edgar was asked to undergo additional training and he began facilitating groups eighteen months later. About ten years ago he became the coordinator of the entire program. Edgar sees his work as a ministry. "Long ago I began to realize that God was using me to give other men the opportunity I had been given to turn their lives around," he said. "I tell these men that change is a lifelong and difficult process but, with treatment and spiritual guidance, it can happen." In addition to the groups he facilitates and the mentoring he offers to other former batterers, Edgar speaks frequently on domestic violence to both religious and secular audiences in his community. He is also a faithful member of his church.

Still, he struggles with his past. "I regret what I've done to cause so many women so much pain," Edgar confessed. "And I've apologized to both my former wives—and also to our children because they too carry the scars from my abusive and violent behavior." But Edgar realizes that apologies alone are not enough. "The destruction I've caused others lets me know that I can't always be trusted," he concluded. "So I continue to work on myself, both spiritually and psychologically. And I ask God to help me to forgive myself—just as I know God has already forgiven me. It's a lifelong process, forgiving one's self. So I'm doing it, one day at a time."

Forms of Abuse, Types of Batterers, and Motivating Factors

Although it may be difficult for some ministers to fathom, there are men worshiping in every congregation with issues similar to those Edgar just discussed. And in order effectively to confront and care for these abusive men, clergypeople must have both a clear understanding of what constitutes abuse and a working knowledge of the factors that motivate perpetrators to victimize the women they claim to love. These are complicated and long-term issues. Therefore, clergypeople should not attempt to deal with them either simplistically or without consulting with people from a variety of professional disciplines.

Forms of Abuse[1]

Domestic violence has many forms, all needing careful study before they can be properly addressed. Complicating matters is the fact that perpetrators usually do not limit themselves to just one type of battering. Let's take a closer look at how some of these forms reveal themselves within the context of an intimate relationship.

Physical Battering

This form of domestic abuse was the one most commonly identified by the clergypeople I interviewed. It was also the type that was easiest for ministers to describe, though there was a tendency on the part of clergy members to limit physical abuse to the sensational acts reported in the media: severe beatings, burnings, chokings, shootings, stabbings, murders. In reality, this type of domestic violence has a very broad scope. "Physical battering has a full range of physical acts," said Dr. L. Kevin Hamberger, a clinical psychologist on the faculty of the Medical College of Wisconsin, Racine Family Practice Residency Program, in Racine, Wisconsin. Since 1983, his primary work has been conducting treatment and research with men who batter their wives and girlfriends. In addition to the acts my clergy colleagues described, Dr. Hamberger identified grabbing, pushing, shoving, slapping, or spitting on one's partner. The goal these men want to achieve is clear: to establish control. "The acts induce fear in victims," Hamberger explained. "Therefore, even if the physical battering is not severe, it still allows abusers to maintain control over their partners."

Sexual Battering

Many clergypeople I interviewed dismissed or minimized the idea of sexual abuse in a marriage. Some ministers, all of them men, did not understand how any husband could ever be accused of raping his wife. These spiritual leaders fail to realize that even in marriage unwanted sexual contact of any nature (not just forced sexual intercourse) is a violation of an individual's right to choose what happens to her own body. Yet, as we saw in chapter 3, several of the men who perpetrate this form of domestic violence use the biblical concept of male headship to justify their actions.

"Sexual battering is a form of physical assault against a victim's body, but it's more specialized in that it involves some kind of sexual contact," explained Dr. Hamberger. He stressed the importance of ministers understanding that this type of domestic violence can be placed on a continuum, from unwanted fondling and touching to forced sexual intercourse. "Just as with physical battering, clergy must keep in mind that even those sexual contacts that might not seem overt or severe can have an extremely powerful and negative effect upon women being abused," Hamberger asserted. "The acts are designed to control and degrade victims."

Property or Pet Destruction

This type of abuse is also physically violent, but it does not involve direct contact with the victim's body. Again, it has a range of manifestations, including such acts as hitting or kicking doors and walls, and killing or threatening to kill the cat, dog, goldfish, and so on. "The power of this form of battering is that it demonstrates the raw, destructive force of a batterer," Hamberger stated. "It's a show of dominance with the abuser communicating to his victim, 'There's no safe place for you to hide. You can lock yourself in the house, but I can break down the door or break out your windows. If I can do this much damage to the walls with my fists, think of what I can do to your body.'" Even if these messages of terror are not spoken by a batterer, Hamberger says, they are still "clearly communicated nonverbally to a victim."

An example of just how powerful the impact property destruction has on a victim can be seen in Debra's story, told in the preceding chapter. Recall the first time she declined to have sex with William, her new husband: he destroyed all the china and crystal Debra had inherited from her grandmother. "William never uttered a sound while he was breaking the items," Debra remembered. "He didn't have to say anything because his unspoken message was loud and clear: he could break me just as easily as he was breaking my china and crystal. So I knew I'd better never refuse to have sex with him again, because I didn't want to end up broken."

Emotional Abuse / Psychological Battering
This form of domestic violence is probably the most difficult for the untrained to understand. Since emotional abuse and psychological battering never leaves physical scars, it is difficult to spot and easy to dismiss. Following are some of the characteristics of men who emotionally abuse their wives. (The same characteristics apply also to men who abuse their girlfriends.)

- He belittles his wife in the company of others and/or in private. He makes snide comments about her intellectual abilities or physical appearance, calling her "dumb," "fat," "ignorant," "naive," "stupid," or "ugly," for example.
- He comments negatively about females in general: less intelligent, more emotional, or inferior to males. Sometimes he'll use derogatory or vulgar terms for women. When challenged about this, the husband will often say he is only joking.
- He does all the talking for the family even in public settings. His wife may defer to her husband before responding to inquiries.
- He quotes biblical passages to support his ordering of the sexes, especially whenever anyone suggests that females are equal to males.

- The wife seems to have no adult relationships or support system outside her husband. Domestic violence flourishes when a woman is isolated from the outside world. An emotionally abusive husband will make every effort to control all aspects of his wife's existence. He'll often force her to keep an account of all her activities, withhold finances, and dictate her relationships.
- The pastor is continually rebuffed when trying to establish a relationship with the family.[2]

Emotional abuse/psychological battering is on a continuum like all other forms of domestic violence. It can also include such behavior as giving looks or gestures, making incessant phone calls to the victim's home or place of work, or stalking. It can also involve more severe kinds of threats. Hamberger explained: "The threats can include such acts as a batterer telling his victim, 'I'm going to kill you'; 'If I can't have you nobody can'; 'I'll never let you go'; 'I'll report you to the welfare office for welfare fraud.'"

Again, one of the primary goals perpetrators of emotional abuse/psychological battering want to achieve is to maintain control over their intimate partners. The effects of this form of domestic violence can be both devastating and long lasting. "Many battered women admit, when all is said and done, that the things that really hurt the most and linger the longest are the wounds that come from psychological battering," Hamberger concluded. "Long after the injuries from physical violence have healed, the pain and uncertainty that result from constant degradation, incessant name calling, and several other emotionally and psychologically abusive acts still remain."

Types of Batterers and Motivating Factors

As stated previously, caring for batterers is a complex and delicate issue, requiring a team of trained professionals from a variety of disciplines. In order for clergypeople to become effective members of this team, we must at the very least have a basic understanding of the various types of batterers and the factors that motivate these men to abuse the women they claim to love. Even after acquiring the necessary training, it is vital that we recognize our limitations. No single individual from any field of study has all the solutions to the complex problems these men face. Ministers therefore should never attempt to deal alone with batterers.

During his many years of research in the field of domestic violence, Hamberger has discovered differences between men who abuse their intimate partners and those who do not. "In general, what we've found in some comparison studies is that men who batter tend to more likely have grown up in homes where they witnessed abuse," Hamberger said. "These men are also slightly more likely to have also been abused themselves. But the greatest contributing factor to their own violent tendencies was for them to have witnessed abuse in their family during childhood." Hamberger has also found that batterers tend to abuse alcohol much more than nonviolent men, and they struggle more with anxiety, depression, and personality disorders.

Psychologist Lenore Walker discussed three types of batterers. The first type are power and control batterers. "These men use violence to obtain and maintain power and control over their women and families," explained Walker, adding that sometimes they use aggression to maintain control over other parts of their world. Walker spoke definitively about how religious teachings can exacerbate the problem. "This is learned behavior and, in my work, I've seen it perpetuated by religious teachings that instruct men to be in control, to be heads of their families. This concept of male dominance doesn't allow women to be who they really are."

The second type of batterer Lenore Walker identified are mentally ill batterers. She called these men "the most neglected batterers," because even if they are ordered into a treatment program, most of the court-ordered programs around the country deal only with power and control issues. "These men not only have a distortion of power and control needs," Walker said, "but they also have a diagnosable mental illness—often mood disorders such as depression, or maybe even obsessive compulsive disorders, anxiety disorders, schizophrenia, etc." Dr. Walker warned that people who provide care to these particular batterers need to be well trained in dealing with various mental illnesses.

The third type of batterer Walker discussed are the anti-social personality disordered and criminally violent men. "In the mental health field, we see them not only committing domestic abuse, but many other kinds of violent and criminal behavior. They're the real sociopaths and psychopaths of society, representing about 20 percent of the population [of batterers]." According to Lenore Walker, this type of batterer cannot be treated in the community. "If we treat them at all—and we don't yet have a successful treatment program—it needs to be where they are unable to harm anybody. They are usually incarcerated."

In their book *When Men Batter Women,* psychologists Neil Jacobson and John Gottman use two other terms to describe men who abuse their intimate partners: pit bulls and cobras. "Cobras appear to be criminal types who have engaged in antisocial behavior since adolescence. They are hedonistic and impulsive. They beat their wives and abuse them emotionally, to stop them from interfering with the cobras' need to get what they want when they want it. Although they may say that they are sorry after a beating and beg their wives' forgiveness, they are usually not sorry. They feel entitled to whatever they want whenever they want it, and try to get it by whatever means necessary."[3]

The authors say that whether cobras are psychopathic or merely antisocial, they are incapable of forming truly intimate relationships with others. "Their wives are convenient stepping-stones to gratification: sex, social status, or economic benefits, for example. But their commitments are superficial, and their stance in the relationship is a 'withdrawing' one. They attempt to keep intimacy to a minimum, and are most likely to be dangerous when their wives attempt to get more from them. They do not fear abandonment, but they will not be controlled. Their own family histories are often chaotic, with neither parent providing love or security, and they were often abused themselves as children."[4]

While cobras are motivated by their desire to get what they want when they want it, pit bulls are motivated by their fear of being left. "The pit bulls are more likely to confine their violence to family members, especially their wives. Their fathers were likely to have battered their mothers, and they have learned that battering is an acceptable way to treat women. But they are not as likely as the cobras to have criminal records or to have been delinquent adolescents. Moreover, even though they batter their wives and abuse them emotionally, unlike the cobras the pit bulls are emotionally dependent on their wives. What they fear most is abandonment. Their fear of abandonment and the desperate need they have not to be abandoned produce jealous rages and attempts to deprive their partners of an independent life. They can be jealous to the point of paranoia, imagining that their wives are having affairs based on clues that most of us would find ridiculous."[5]

Jacobson and Gottman say that although both cobras and pit bulls dominate their wives and have great control needs, the motivating factors in these two types of batterers are different. "The pit bulls are motivated by fear of being left, while cobras are motivated by a desire to get as much immediate gratification as possible."[6] The authors warn that both groups of men are very dangerous when they feel threatened. "The pit bulls, although somewhat less violent in general than the cobras, are also capable of severe assault and murder, just as the cobras are. Although one is safer trying to leave a pit bull in the short run, pit bulls may actually be more dangerous to leave in the long run. Cobras strike swiftly and with great lethality when they feel threatened, but they are also easily distracted after those initial strikes and move on to other targets. In contrast, pit bulls sink their teeth into their targets; once they sink their teeth into you, it is hard to get them to let go!"[7]

Can Abusive Men Change?

Having looked at some of the forms of abuse, types of abusers, and some of the factors that motivate men to attack their intimate partners, let us now turn our attention to the question at the head of this chapter: Once an abuser, always an abuser?

Lasting change is difficult for most people. Those of us who have struggled with keeping our weight down, for instance, know that it's much easier to lose pounds than to keep them off in the long run. Former cigarette smokers and alcohol or drug users often hang onto the credo "One day at a time" to help them in their struggle to break free permanently from these behaviors. For the men who abuse and batter their intimate partners, attaining lasting change can be even more tenuous. "The problem with violence is that it is quite effective in the short-term for getting what the perpetrator wants when he wants it," said Dr. Lenore Walker. She thinks abusive men can change, but that it's a difficult process. "Other methods of persuasion take longer and require much more effort on the short-term, but are far more effective over the long-term for maintenance. However, it is difficult to put off short-term gratification when you are not even sure that you will get what you want [in the long-term]."

Several of the people I interviewed—victims and even some of the professionals working with batterers—told me they have strong doubts about permanent change in perpetrators. But, like Lenore Walker, several other professionals working in the field say that lasting change, though an arduous task, can definitely be achieved. If they believed otherwise, these professionals said emphatically, they would not be involved in the care of abusers. I, too, strongly believe in the ability of perpetrators of domestic violence to change permanently their abusive and violent ways. Like so many other caregivers, if I thought otherwise I would not be working with these men or in the Christian ministry. My faith is solidly rooted in the belief that God can change anyone. The Hebrew and Christian Scriptures are replete with stories of how faith in God and Jesus Christ changed the lives of countless women and men. All things are possible with God, the Bible tells me. Therefore, I believe that men who abuse and batter their intimate partners can change provided these men commit themselves to the long-term dedication and effort that change requires.

Now that I've expressed one of the most fundamental truths of my Christian faith, let me discuss where my caution lies. It's been my experience that lasting change, especially from a Christian viewpoint, requires several things. A vital first step is repentance—showing remorse over our sins, taking full responsibility for the damage we've caused others, and being willing to work on correcting any inappropriate behavior so that we won't repeat our harmful actions. Perpetrators of domestic abuse usually fall short of that. They rarely take responsibility for the destruction they've caused, blaming instead alcohol, children, drugs, job stresses, mood swings, and, especially, their victims.[8]

"Batterers frequently tell me that their wives are the cause of their abusive behavior," said Melody Moody, a social worker at Marine Corps Base Hawaii in Kaneohe Bay, Hawaii. One of Moody's primary tasks is to deal with incidents of domestic violence among military families. She facilitates treatment programs with perpetrators and support groups for victims. "Abusers will use whatever justification they can grab hold of," Moody insisted. "They'll say that their wives are to blame for their own victimization because 'she just pushed and pushed and pushed until I snapped' or 'you don't understand how awful and outrageous she is to live with' or 'she's having an affair.'" Moody stated that even men who say they have no spiritual belief system will still use the Christian Scriptures to justify their abusive behaviors when it is convenient for them. "They'll tell me, 'According to the Bible, I'm the head of my wife, the boss. So I can't let her do the things she's been doing, because she'll start thinking she's the boss.'"

Despite the blaming and justifying, Moody, who is herself a Christian, believes in God's ability to change anybody, including perpetrators of domestic violence, but she also thinks that lasting change will not occur without a lot of dedication and hard work. "Some of the guys in our program have no intention of changing," Moody said. "They go through group putting in their time and saying whatever they think people want to hear. And, after their weeks are up, these men go on doing what they darn well please." Moody said, however, that she has witnessed some of the other men making definite, positive changes. "They work very hard on their issues and commit themselves to a new and more healthy lifestyle. And these men recognize change is a long and often difficult journey."

L. Kevin Hamberger, who is a Christian as well, also believes that perpetrators can change, but thinks this is a lifelong process. "I think that it's an awful lot to expect a twelve-, twenty-four-, or even a fifty-week program to get a person to completely turn their whole life around, to come out very different than they were before: egalitarian, totally respectful, totally nonabusive, and nonviolent in their lives from that point forward," Hamberger contended. One of the most positive benefits of treatment groups, he said, is to put an abuser in a position to make some quick changes to quell the immediate crisis and turmoil of battering. Then, after he's completed treatment, the perpetrator can continue to work on changing throughout the rest of his life. "I do think for many batterers this process of change will involve them working the rest of their lives on their issues," Dr. Hamberger concluded.

I asked Edgar, the man whose story was told earlier in this chapter, his thoughts on abusive men changing. It's been more than fifteen years, Edgar said, since he's physically abused any woman. He also continues abiding by his goal of not perpetrating emotional, physical, psychological, or sexual abuse. And it's been almost as much time since Edgar completed treatment, rededicated his life to Christ, and began attending a weekly support group with other former batterers, and since he became the coordinator of a large batterers' intervention program. "First of all, I don't buy the concept of once an abuser, always an abuser," Edgar stated categorically. "I do think a statement like 'Once an abuser, the capacity to abuse again' would be far more accurate. However, I know for a fact that an abuser's behavior can change. If I didn't believe this, I couldn't be doing the work I'm doing."

Edgar disclosed that there are men who have been through treatment in his program with whom he has established a camaraderie. "I know not only these men, but also their wives and families," he said. "I believe they've made some significant positive changes in their lives—not because the men themselves claim this, but because over a long period of time their wives and family members also say these men have changed. And, personally, I've witnessed a change in the attitude, behavior, countenance, and values of some former batterers. So, without a doubt, I know change happens."

Regarding himself, Edgar is even more clear: change for him will be a lifelong spiritual and psychological process. "My first of many 'cleansings' occurred when I finally confessed my sins to God and took full responsibility for all of the hurt I caused," Edgar said. Over time, however, he began to realize this was only the beginning of his long journey. "I had to also work on my issues, both psychologically and spiritually, to ensure that I wouldn't fall back on my former destructive ways," he said. "It's easy to say 'I'm a changed man,' but far more difficult to do all of the necessary work to effect lasting change."

One of the differences Edgar now sees in himself centers around his attitude toward women. He says Christianity has helped him to achieve an egalitarian view of men and women. "Jesus is my model, and Jesus didn't degrade or abuse women in any way," he said. "I used to devalue women, treating them as inferior to men and using females as objects to satisfy my sexual desires. This was sinful on my part and it demonstrates the disrespect I once had in my heart toward women and myself. The difference now is that I'm guided by Christ. He always treats humans, females and males, with love and respect."

Despite having the assurance that he's been redeemed by the love and power of Jesus Christ, Edgar still describes his process of change as a lifelong one. "I know I could abuse again because I've been down that evil road before," Edgar stated matter-of-factly. "So I choose to see my journey of change as everlasting. I don't want my arrogance or ego to get in the way, to put me back on the cold and dark path of sin and destruction. Therefore, I take life one day at a time: living by the Christian principles of love and respect for all of humankind, attending a weekly support group with other former batterers, worshiping regularly at my church, and being guided by the one who freed me from bondage—Christ Jesus."

What Clergypeople Need to Know to Care for Abusers

Fred, a colleague and fellow Christian, visited my office three weeks after Heather, his wife of eleven years, decided to separate from him. The reason for her decision, Fred readily disclosed, was because of his emotional and physical attacks on her. Distraught and expressing remorse, the thirty-eight-year-old father of four sons sobbed openly as he sat in the chair across from me. "It's all my fault," Fred whispered, referring to why Heather had decided to take their children and settle into temporary housing at a nearby shelter for abused and battered women. "I was pretty mean to Heather, at times my behavior was both disgusting and sinful. But those days are all behind me now. God has opened my eyes and heart and changed my wicked ways. I'll never, ever hurt Heather again."

I asked Fred what steps he was taking to ensure he'd maintain his commitment to change. "God has replaced my arrogant and controlling nature with his gentle and sweet spirit," Fred testified. God could undoubtedly change any human, I responded. But I also believed that change was a long-term process. I told Fred he needed both abuser treatment and spiritual counseling. In addition to seeing me, I encouraged him to seek help from either a batterers' program or a therapist who was trained specifically to work with men who abuse their partners. Fred rejected both of my suggestions. "There's no need for treatment groups or therapists when God has a hold of you," he snapped. "God has changed me already."

Ministers need to know that perpetrators of domestic violence can be very manipulative, even charming. They will tell friends, professionals, strangers, and, particularly, the women they abuse exactly what the abusers think others want to hear. Clergypeople, in my opinion, are especially naive about abusers' claims to be "changed by God." Believing that God can indeed change people, and often lacking the proper training to deal with abusers, we easily fall for perpetrators' slick talk and persuasive powers.

Let's say, for example, an abuser in your congregation attends only a few support group meetings for abusive and violent men. Or he suddenly confesses his sins in front of the congregation, apologizing (with a full complement of emotions!) to his wife and children, and promising never to abuse anyone again. Don't be fooled. Yes, I believe God can change humans. Often, though, abusers' claims of change are simply another link in the chain of violence—the abuser violates his wife, expresses deep remorse to her in letters, with flowers, and over fancy dinners, and makes an ostensibly sincere promise to change. But he refuses to seek (or stay in) treatment, and, within weeks, months, and perhaps years, the cycle begins again. Lasting change, both spiritual and psychological, takes time and hard work.[9]

Nanci Kreidman knows all about the many cautions that must be taken in dealing with abusive men who claim to have changed. The executive director of the Domestic Violence Clearinghouse and Legal Hotline, an agency located on Oahu that serves victims of domestic violence through a variety of direct services, began running the first batterers' program in Hawaii in the late 1970s. "Over the years I dealt with lots of batterers who had been ordered into group," Kreidman reflected. "At first, these men did a lot of blaming, denying, and resisting. Then, like clockwork, many of them would suddenly announce a belief in God and they'd claim everything was OK." Kreidman tried to keep a positive outlook about the faith these men said they possessed. "I always wanted to acknowledge their spiritual discovery," she said. "But I also wanted to know what skills the men were learning, and how they thought these skills would help prevent them from repeating the behaviors that got them into trouble in the first place."

Kreidman is especially concerned about what she calls "pastoral care in a vacuum," spiritual support provided by clergypeople who not only lack proper training to care for batterers and victims, but who refuse to refer batterers to trained professionals. "Spiritual leaders need to know that this style of pastoral care is dangerous," Kreidman said. "If the authority figure—which is how most people in a congregation view pastors—says to a victim, 'Your husband is a changed man. God has taken away his abusive and violent tendencies and it's now safe for you to return home to your husband,' then the victim is going to think that all her husband's problems are solved. As a result of this poor advice, many women go back into potentially lethal situations."

Nancy Murphy is the executive director of the Northwest Family Life Learning and Counseling Center, a Christian organization in Seattle certified by the State of Washington to provide treatment to perpetrators of domestic violence. She expressed similar concerns about how clergy members are often deceived by abusers claiming to be changed by God, and is even more troubled when ministers unwittingly set victims up as culprits. "Too many clergy, after hearing the testimony of a perpetrator who has supposedly changed, will quickly turn around and applaud the guy for his confession," Murphy said. "It's as though pastors are saying to the victim, 'Look at this guy, he's really a man with a heart after God.' The strong implication is that the woman needs to take this man back immediately. If she doesn't, then she's looked at as the person with the problem."

How, then, can clergypeople care effectively for perpetrators of domestic violence? What steps do we need to take to avoid the many pitfalls an abuser will place before us, such as blaming his victim, manipulation, slick talk, and an early proclamation of being changed by God? Here are some approaches for ministers to consider:

• *Seek training.* There is no substitute for proper education. Domestic violence training, taken in conferences, workshops, and videos and by reading articles, pamphlets, and books on the subject will greatly reduce the temptation of spiritual caregivers to offer poor or quick-fix advice.

• *Know your limits.* No single person, not even those who have worked against domestic violence for decades, has the knowledge and training to deal with all the complexities associated with caring for perpetrators. As ministers, we must not go beyond our level of training. Otherwise, we will end up causing more harm than good and might even make a victim's situation more dangerous, even lethal. In addition, as we'll discuss further in chapter 6, clergy members must be willing to work in collaboration with other professionals. We must share our spiritual expertise with attorneys, advocacy workers, group facilitators, law enforcement officers, psychologists, social workers, and other caregivers, and make referrals to these professionals.

• *Avoid bringing the abuser together with the victim to "get at the truth."* Remember, perpetrators are often deceitful and manipulative. They may behave appropriately (even charmingly) in the pastor's office, but then further punish their wives or girlfriends when they get home. (Refer to chapter 2 for more information on this matter.)

• *Be realistic.* Ultimately, there are no foolproof plans to keep a woman totally safe from her abusive partner—even if that partner is confronted, seeks treatment, or says he is "a changed man." Nonetheless, clergypeople can take the following steps to make a victim's safety more likely:

1. Never confront an abusive man without thoroughly discussing with his intimate partner both the benefits and the potential risks that such a confrontation could bring.
2. Make sure the victim has a safety plan (such as the one discussed in chapter 2) that can be implemented quickly should her partner's abuse continue or escalate.

• P*ut the victim's safety first.* Although caring for an abuser is part of our responsibility as Christian leaders, our primary focus must always be to ensure the safety of a victim and her children. As we discussed in chapter 2, too many clergypeople addressing situations of domestic violence list "saving the marriage" and "keeping the family together" as their top priorities. But these goals should only be considered after perpetrators receive both abuser treatment and spiritual counseling. Even then ministers must determine, with reasonable certainty, that the perpetrator's abuse and violence have completely stopped before suggesting to a victim that she return to her victimizer. Ultimately, however, even if the relationship becomes totally free from abuse, the decision to stay or leave the perpetrator must be left up to the victim.

• *Hold him accountable.* Remember, perpetrators of domestic violence rarely take responsibility for their destruction. Instead they blame alcohol, children, drugs, job stresses, mood swings, Satan, and, especially, their victims. Abusers will also minimize the hurt they've caused their victims, making excuses such as, "I only shook my wife; it's not like I beat her with my fists"; "I've called her a 'bitch' and 'slut,' but only once or twice during our entire marriage"; and "Sure, I asked my wife to keep an account of all her activities, but that's only because I love her so much."

Clergypeople must not be taken in by an abuser's manipulative ways and inappropriate justifications. While it is important for pastors to affirm the love, forgiveness, and healing that Christ offers, it is vital to challenge the perpetrator to take responsibility for his abuse and to encourage him to seek treatment. That will require a pastor regularly and gently to ask the perpetrator how he plans to get better: "What step have you taken recently to get help for how you treat your wife? Have you seen a counselor? Have you joined a treatment group?"[10]

• *Redirect his Scripture reading.* For ongoing spiritual care, I recommend that pastors set up with the abuser a reading schedule of passages from Scripture that teach equal value and dignity of husband and wife. Then pastor and abuser can discuss the larger theological dimensions of how God views men and women. That can counterbalance the tendency by abusers to misquote biblical texts to support male dominance. Here are a few passages that I've found helpful: Genesis 1:26-28; 1 Corinthians 7:3-4 and 11:11-12; Galatians 5:13; Ephesians 5:21 and 5:25-33; and Philippians 2:3.[11]

• *Hold out hope.* That means simply saying that if the abuser wants to change and will do the hard work, he can change, that with God anything is possible. That's the promise of the gospel. Through prayer, Scripture reading, spiritual counseling, and batterers' treatment, an abuser can become whole.[12]

Conclusion

Perpetrators of domestic violence are everywhere; some even worship in and lead our churches. There are men who praise God and preach Jesus who also beat, control, curse, rape, and terrorize their wives and girlfriends. These men seldom take responsibility for their abuse, blaming instead everything from the alcohol they consume and the drugs they take, to Satan, their children, and jobs. Most often, however, these men blame the very women they attack. Abusers often refuse to seek (or stay in) batterers' treatment programs or spiritual counseling; many claim, after a very short period of time, to be "a man changed by God." But lasting change, both spiritually and psychologically, seldom occurs without hard work over a long period of time.

Clergypeople have done a poor job in holding perpetrators accountable for the pain they've caused. Lacking the appropriate training to understand the dynamics of battering, and demonstrating resistance to working collaboratively with other professionals, ministers are often deceived by the smooth and manipulative testimonies of abusers proclaiming divine transformation. At times, clergy members even conjoin with batterers and blame women for their own victimization. "He said he was sorry, and his confession made the entire congregation cry," one pastor told me regarding an abuser who was worshiping in his church. "So I encouraged his wife to give him a second chance. 'To err is human, to forgive is divine,' I told the wife. So she took him back, but, within a month, this same man nearly beat her to death. I still feel guilty, knowing that my poor advice almost cost a woman her life."

Perpetrators of domestic violence can change, but few can do so without a long-term commitment to work on their issues. Clergy and other pastoral ministers can assist abusers in this difficult but necessary process. For us to be effective in our efforts, however, we must obtain domestic violence training and learn the various dynamics that compel men to abuse and batter their intimate partners. Ministers must also be willing to work closely with professionals from a variety of other disciplines. Without taking these vital steps, clergypeople will be helpful to neither victims nor to the men who abuse them.

Questions for Discussion

1. What did you feel and think as you read Edgar's story? Discuss the parts of the story with which you identify. Do you think Edgar has really changed? If you answered yes, how would you as a minister help him avoid returning to his abusive past?

2. List and describe the forms of battering discussed in the chapter. Have you known anyone who has used these forms on an intimate partner? If yes, how did you deal with this situation?

3. Discuss the types of batterers described in the chapter. What insights did you gain by reading about these men? What do perpetrators want to accomplish by engaging in abuse? Do you think you are qualified to minister to abusers? If not, what else do you need to become qualified?

4. Are there men in your congregation who abuse and batter their wives or girlfriends? How have you confronted and ministered to these hurtful men?

5. Would you be willing to work in collaboration with psychologists, social workers, and other professionals in your community to ensure the safety of women and children, and also to help abusers learn healthier ways of dealing with their problems? What would you see as your role in this collaborative effort?

6. List and discuss five approaches clergy and other pastoral workers can take to become more effective caregivers to men who abuse and batter their wives and girlfriends.

Chapter 5. The Thorny Question of Forgiveness

When my pastors and church friends found out that Edward and I were separated, and even though they knew it was because of his violence, one of the very first reactions from everybody in the church was,"Well, you need to forgive him."Their response was devastating to me. It was as if what they knew about my husband's abuse didn't matter. "Forgive and forget," they said. I couldn't do either at the time, so I felt like such a sinner.

—MARY, DOMESTIC VIOLENCE SURVIVOR

Forgiveness is a complex issue, both psychologically and spiritually, for survivors of domestic violence. This is especially the case for victims who were raised in the Christian faith. (The same is true of survivors from several other faith groups, but we'll focus here on Christianity.) Pastors, church members, family, and friends tell victims that forgiveness is a virtuous act, necessary for keeping them in harmony with God, Jesus, others, and themselves. Survivors also hear that forgiveness will make everything OK (therefore, they should forget the pain their perpetrators caused); forgiveness will "save" their marriages and families; and if survivors don't forgive, God will not forgive them of their own transgressions. (Distressingly, ministers seldom mention the transgressions perpetrated by batterers!) This poor and usually unsolicited advice leaves many victims feeling a great deal of pressure to return to, or remain in, unhealthy and dangerous marriages.

Consider the story of Mary. We first read about her twelve-year marriage to Edward, a Christian minister, in chapter 3. Edward repeatedly tortured his wife in emotional, physical, and sexual ways.

But when Mary disclosed her husband's abusive behavior to the other pastors and several laypeople of the church, she was rebuked for separating from him. "When my pastors and church friends found out that Edward and I were separated, and even though they knew it was because of his violence, one of the very first reactions from everybody in the church was, 'Well, you need to forgive him,'" Mary recalled. "Their response was devastating to me. It was as if what they knew about my husband's abuse didn't matter. 'Forgive and forget,' they all said. I couldn't do either at the time, so I felt like such a sinner."

What is forgiveness—and what is it not? What do the Christian Scriptures teach us about this concept? How can ministers help victims who struggle with the thorny question of forgiveness?

To help us address these questions I will draw on the insights of experts from a wide variety of fields. I have also gathered firsthand data from survivors themselves. As is the case in other parts of the book, most of the survivors quoted in this chapter are identified by a pseudonym and certain aspects of their stories have been changed to maintain their anonymity and safety.

Let us start by considering the story of Cynthia, who was married for sixteen years to Bob, a Christian minister.

Cynthia's Story

"Bob would always tell me that unless I forgave him, God wouldn't forgive my sins," recalled Cynthia, looking back on her marriage to a man who repeatedly abused her. "He'd say I was to forgive him immediately and never bring up any of the episodes of abuse again. This would allow our marriage to remain strong and free from Satan, Bob told me. But how could I forgive or forget my husband's actions when he kept abusing me? And why was a Christian man, the senior pastor of a church no less, battering his wife?"

The couple married in 1975. Cynthia said Bob's public and private personae were as different as night and day. "At church and in the community he was admired by everyone," she said. "Bob seemed to be a kind and loving man who'd praise me from the pulpit on a regular basis for the love and financial support I provided as he pursued a doctoral degree in psychology. 'My wife is God's greatest gift to me,' he would say. 'She's not only beautiful and intelligent, but also such a wonderful mother to our daughter. I don't know what I'd do without her.'"

But at home, Cynthia said Bob showed another side. "He treated me and eventually our daughter like we were his research subjects. Any time I'd offer an opinion different than his he'd roll his eyes and belittle me. While Bob told everyone out in public that I was such a good wife, in the privacy of our home he'd berate me constantly. 'Look, you're an OK businesswoman, but you know nothing about theology and psychology,' he'd coldly remind me. When my opinions proved to be correct, Bob would abuse me even further. 'So you made a lucky guess, you highly educated bitch,' he'd shout. 'But only a bride of Satan's would make her husband look stupid in front of other people.'"

Bob also began using a phrase that Cynthia said caused her the greatest hurt. "When he'd become really enraged—which occurred more and more frequently and for no apparent reason—my husband would yell, 'Fuck you!' Once he found out how much these words hurt and humiliated me, Bob used the phrase all the time. This was my husband, mind you, a Christian pastor and the father of my little girl, shouting 'Fuck you' to the woman he'd vowed to always love and respect. I felt demoralized."

Cynthia says her spirit reached an even lower ebb when Bob's emotional and psychological battering started also to include episodes of physical violence. "I tended to play down Bob's physical abuse back then because it was atypical of what I was reading about physically abusive men," Cynthia admitted. "There was no identifiable cycle. Instead, Bob would hit me once or twice a year. Now I can also see how damaging his physical battering was to my emotional, psychological, and spiritual well-being."

Bob first physically abused his wife during the second year of their marriage. "Our daughter was a newborn, not even a month old at the time," Cynthia recounted. "It was early on a Sunday morning.

I'd just nursed the baby and asked Bob to hold her while I took a quick shower and dressed for church. Well, our daughter threw up all over Bob's shirt and tie. He went into a rampage." Accusing his wife of subconsciously "willing" their infant daughter to vomit on him, Bob marched into the bathroom and demanded that Cynthia come out of the shower immediately to clean his soiled clothing. "I remember thinking how childish Bob was acting, he was yelling at the top of his lungs," noted Cynthia. "It was only a little vomit, and my husband must have had at least twenty other clean shirts and ties in his closet. So I asked Bob to give me a moment to rinse the shampoo out of my hair. The next thing I knew he had stepped into the tub of running water, fully dressed, and was throwing me through the sliding glass doors of our shower." Cynthia ended up lying in a pool of her own blood. A huge bump developed on the side of her head after she hit it on the tile floor.

Devastated and crying hysterically, Cynthia felt trapped. "I was both humiliated and terrified, but I knew I wouldn't tell a soul what Bob had done. My parents taught me to deal with personal problems inside the home and, besides, I didn't want anybody to think badly of my minister husband." Bob apologized to Cynthia for his physical violence. But he took no responsibility for it. "He said if I hadn't 'willed' our daughter to vomit on him, then he wouldn't have thrown me through the glass," Cynthia explained. "Bob even went so far as to say I hit my head on the tile floor because I must have wanted to get a bruise, in order to make people think that he was a wife beater. I thought this reasoning was absolutely insane, but I said nothing at the time." Bob also told his battered wife it was Satan working inside his soul that caused the abuse. "It was everyone's fault except his own," Cynthia recalled ruefully.

As Bob always did after he abused Cynthia, the minister insisted that his wife forgive him. Cynthia vividly recalled what her husband did as she lay naked and bleeding on the cold tile floor. "Bob ran out to the bookshelf, came back into the bathroom with a Bible, and started quoting Scripture: 'For if you forgive men when they sin against you, your heavenly Father will also forgive you. But if you do not forgive men their sins, your Father will not forgive your sins'"

[Matthew 6:14-15 NIV]. He also told Cynthia that if she didn't forgive him, she was not practicing Christian love. Cynthia felt even more agonized and confused.

"I knew Bob's behavior wasn't right, especially his constant emotional and psychological berating of me," Cynthia confessed. "But I kept blaming myself: 'Maybe I should have kept my mouth shut here, or not done that there'—typical behavior for a victim, I now realize. So after my husband the minister started telling me I had to forgive and forget the abuse, I felt I had no choice. Each time he'd abuse me and demand absolution I'd say to Bob, 'I forgive you.'" Cynthia also promised, at her husband's insistence, never again to mention any of the abusive episodes. She now admits she did this only to keep the peace. "Bob never took responsibility for his behavior. Instead, he'd always blame me, our child, and Satan: 'It's not me who's saying and doing these terrible things to you,' he'd claim, 'It's man's dark side, Satan, who's causing all of this evil behavior to appear.' Still, Bob demanded that I forgive and forget all the hurt he was perpetrating in order to reconcile our marriage. I didn't know what to do or where to turn."

What Is Forgiveness—and What Is It Not?

In order for clergypeople to help victims of domestic violence come to terms with the issue of forgiveness, clergy must first have an accurate understanding of what forgiveness is—and what it is not.

Forgiveness is the decision on the part of a person who has been abused, betrayed, or wronged to let go of, or put aside, the justifiable anger, bitterness, and hurt that arises from being victimized. Curtiss Paul DeYoung writes: "The decision to forgive or seek forgiveness is ours. With God it is always reciprocal. We ask God to be forgiven and we are—fully and unconditionally—but this may not happen in our human relationships. Forgiveness, though, does not hinge upon whether we gain the response we seek. Forgiveness is a healing act, releasing the pain that comes from anger or fear. [I]t allows us to refocus our anger on injustice rather than on the perpetrator(s) of injustice."[1]

Although victims may be pressured by clergy and congregants to forgive instantaneously, forgiveness is usually a very long and arduous process. "The correlation between the intensity of the hurt and the length of time a victim needs to work through it has to be carefully considered," asserts Rev. Fritz Fritschel, the assisting pastor at the Lutheran Church of Honolulu, a congregation of the Evangelical Lutheran Church in America. He has worked actively for a number of years to increase public awareness of domestic violence. "In situations of domestic violence, for example, the hurt is often ongoing and perpetrated for years," explained Fritschel. "Therefore, it's unrealistic to think that forgiveness, under these circumstances, will be a short-term process."

Rev. Joan Ishibashi, a United Church of Christ minister also serving in Honolulu, knows firsthand about how forgiveness may require time. As will be detailed in the next chapter, for two years while attending college she dated a man who battered her physically, psychologically, and sexually. "I've forgiven my ex-boyfriend, but it took a very long time," Ishibashi declared. "I started to realize that the forgiveness was for me as much as for him. So rather than trying to suppress the pain from his abuse like I'd done for years, I told myself I needed to dig it out of me. And once the memories began to come to the surface, I knew I had to work through them in order to let them go and get on with my life." Ishibashi says one of the steps that helped her let go was the effort to understand her offender. "Over time, I began attempting to gain insight into why my ex-boyfriend was the way he was, while still holding him responsible for his behavior. For instance, I looked at the way he was raised and the messages he received from his parents about females. This helped me release my anger and bitterness. Nevertheless, it took a long, long time to forgive him for all the hurt he caused me."

Forgiveness in the New Testament

Most Christians are taught from an early age by parents, pastors, Sunday school teachers, and others about the many blessings that result from granting and receiving forgiveness. We are also told of

the negative consequences that will occur if we choose not to forgive. A cherished virtue, forgiveness is held in the same regard as the
three virtues that Christians are told will abide forever: faith, hope,
and love. "Forgiveness has a history. Much of that history derives
from Hebrew roots and Scriptures. Christians have adopted those
roots and grafted on some nuances from the New Testament and
myriad later references," wrote Martin E. Marty in *Dimensions of
Forgiveness.*[2] Christians hold forgiveness in such high esteem because
of the way that biblical examples have been interpreted to them. But
how was forgiveness understood in the first century? Were there
circumstances when forgiveness was viewed as inappropriate? What
do these ancient teachings about forgiveness have to tell us regarding twenty-first-century living, particularly as it relates to our pastoral care of victims of domestic violence?

Forgiveness has a very important role in Christendom. Most of
us raised in the Christian faith grew up hearing about the forgiving
nature of the divine. Martin E. Marty stated, "One is called to the
Christian community or church to experience forgiveness from God
and a consequent awareness and reality of a 'new creation' or 'the
new being.' The consequence of this experience is that the divine
version somehow inspires forgiveness among humans."[3] Jesus himself places a high value on forgiveness. Marty continued: "The
Sermon on the Mount frames sayings of Jesus as calling for forgiveness and commanding that disciples should not judge others
(Matthew 5–7; see specifically Matthew 5:21-26, 6:9-15, 7:1-5). In
the Lord's Prayer (Matthew 6:9-13), the mirror, impulse, and
instrument for prayer by the community, forgiving is the *only* human
action; the rest of the prayer calls for God to act apart from human
participation."[4] In addition, Jesus modeled forgiveness throughout
his ministry. However, the so-called act of forgiveness that leaves
victims vulnerable to further abuse from violent men is not something that Jesus would condone.

A common controversy arises today when people try to explore
the New Testament perspective of forgiveness: namely, whether
repentance must precede forgiveness. In the book *Violence against
Women and Children,* Frederick Keene takes a close look at the

debate. "The first position [that repentance is required for forgiveness] usually is regarded as one taken by more 'conservative' Christians and, biblically, is based on such texts as Mark 1:4 (NRSV):

> John the baptizer appeared in the wilderness, proclaiming a baptism of repentance (metanoia) for the forgiveness (aphesis) of sins.

The second position usually is regarded as more 'liberal,' and finds its biblical roots in passages such as Mark 2:1-12, especially Mark 2:5 (NRSV):

> When Jesus saw their faith, he said to the paralytic, 'Son, your sins are forgiven (aphiēmi).'"[5]

The issue of whether forgiveness requires repentance—either before forgiveness is offered or in order for it to be accepted—was not the concern in the New Testament world of the first century. Instead the writers gave primary attention to such matters as who forgave, who was forgiven, and the nature of the relationship between the people involved. In the first-century Mediterranean world, one person forgiving another was deemed appropriate only if the forgiver were in a higher socioeconomic position than the forgiven, and hence in a position to act as a patron.[6] An offer of forgiveness in that society was a challenge to the honor of the person being forgiven, at least in the case of a male recipient.[7] Keene notes, "Such a challenge from an inferior would be an insult, but from a superior or an equal could be accepted. It would depend on how it were proffered."[8]

The ancient world's cultural-anthropological view of forgiveness had profound implications for the New Testament's perspective. Keene elaborates: "[I]t is not possible from the point of view of the New Testament for one person to forgive another person of greater power. This would mean that if a tenant has a grievance against a landlord as part of their landlord/tenant relationship, the tenant not only is not called upon to forgive, but in fact cannot forgive the landlord so long as that relationship exists—and this is independent of whether or not the landlord 'makes restitution.' It would also mean that if a man beats his wife, the battered woman not only is not required to forgive her husband, but in fact should not forgive him so long as the hierarchical power relationship exists within the marriage. The tenant can forgive a financial wrong only of a financial equal (or inferior). A wife can forgive a marital wrong only as a marital equal."[9] Because domestic violence, by definition, establishes an imbalance of power in a marriage, clergy should never encourage abused wives to forgive the husbands who violate them. Rather, spiritual leaders must help victims focus on their own need for healing, safety, and self-care.

There are three Greek words used in the New Testament for the verb "to forgive": *aphiēmi* with its associated noun *aphesis; charizomai;* and *apoluō. Apoluō* occurs in the sense of "to forgive" only in Luke 6:37 (twice). It usually means to dismiss or to divorce; it is used in Matthew 5:32 in the pronouncements on divorce. In the New Testament world, where marriages were patriarchal relationships dominated by husbands, only a man could initiate a divorce. This context suggests that in Luke 6:37 forgiveness can come only from the more powerful person (the husband).[10]

The predominant verbs of forgiveness are *aphiēmi* and *charizomai. Aphiēmi* and its associated noun *aphesis* have two basic, related meanings. The first is an essentially juridical meaning of "to leave" or "to release." Luke 4:18 (NRSV) states: "He has sent me to proclaim release (*aphiēmi*) to the captives." This can be extended also to many cases in which someone or something is leaving. For example, in Mark 1:18 (NRSV) we read about the story of the earliest disciples leaving their livelihood to follow Jesus: "And immediately they left (*aphiēmi*) their nets and followed him." The other meaning of *aphiēmi* is essentially commercial: to remit or forgive, especially a debt. This carries over from both common Greek usage and the Septuagint, and can be seen in Matthew 6:12 (NRSV): "And forgive (*aphiēmi*) us our debts, as we also have forgiven (*aphiēmi*) our debtors."[11]

The verb *charizomai* is almost exclusively Pauline. In the New Testament, it occurs only in Luke, Paul, and the deutero-Pauline literature. In Luke, it usually refers to favors granted to someone. For example, Acts 4:14 says that Barabbas was released as a favor to the people: "But you rejected the Holy and Righteous One and asked to have a murderer given (*charizomai*) to you." *Charizomai,* to give freely, is from the same root as *charis,* which is the word usually translated as "grace" in Pauline literature.[12]

The vast majority of New Testament references to forgiveness refer to God's forgiveness of sins, Jesus' forgiving of another's sins, or, especially after the Resurrection, a blending of these two categories in which God's forgiveness is mediated in some way by Jesus.[13] The New Testament makes relative few references to forgiveness, most dealing with either juridical or commercial situations. Frederick Keene observes, "All of these references are of necessity hierarchical: within the context of the New Testament, God and Jesus are always in a (or the) position of power with regard to sin. Furthermore, the words used are almost always *aphiēmi* or *aphesis,* giving this forgiveness of sin juridical or commercial overtones. When it comes to people forgiving other people, there are not very many references. When Synoptic parallels are taken together, there are seven such references in the gospels, and four in the epistolary literature."[14]

The above lessons are important for ministers to remember if we are to provide effective pastoral care to survivors of domestic violence struggling with the thorny question of forgiveness. Sometimes our attempts to integrate first-century practices betray our ignorance of the New Testament's historical context. As a result, we can end up causing more harm than good. Forgiveness is an invaluable aspect of a survivor's healing process. But ministers must never pressure an abused woman into forgiving her offender—especially if we are drawing some New Testament scripture out of its proper context.

Common but Inaccurate Equations

Professional caregivers, laypeople, and victims' family members and friends often equate forgiveness with forgetting, reconciliation, and the notion that the victim should somehow view the abuse as being either not so bad or even acceptable. These misguided opinions have made it more difficult for survivors to break free of partners who are dangerous and sometimes even lethal. Let's take a closer look at each of the equations.

Forgiveness as Reconciliation

While forgiveness and reconciliation are closely linked in New Testament theology, it is important for clergypeople and other Christians to understand that forgiveness and reconciliation are not one and the same. As stated earlier, forgiveness is a decision on the part of someone who has been wronged to let go or put aside anger, bitterness, hurt, and the desire for retaliation against or punishment of the transgressor. It is a choice that can be made only by the victimized. Reconciliation, on the other hand, is a decision made by both victim and perpetrator(s). It is the restoration of a relationship that has been broken by abuse, betrayal, and other wrongs. "Ultimately, the thing which seems to be a sticking point with people in the area of abuse is that they confuse the concept of forgiveness with the concept of reconciliation," said Dr. Everett L. Worthington, Jr., a clinical psychologist and professor at Virginia Commonwealth University. He is a Christian and a pioneer in the field of the scientific study of forgiveness. "Some victims think if we suggest that they consider forgiveness, we're telling them they ought to get back into or reconcile an abusive relationship, ought to not protect themselves, and that the abuse is something that is beyond and gone. But this is not really what forgiveness is. Forgiveness is something that a person grants to another person. It's a gift. Reconciliation is something that's an interpersonal happening. It involves two people, not one. Furthermore, you don't grant reconciliation, you earn reconciliation. Reconciliation is needed when trust has been broken in a relationship, which has happened in domestic abuse situations. And reconciliation is a restoration of that trust, through mutually trustworthy behavior."

Equating forgiveness with reconciliation can be especially detrimental to victims of domestic violence. As noted in the preceding chapter, perpetrators rarely take responsibility for their abusive behavior. Instead, they blame alcohol, drugs, children, job stresses, mood swings, Satan, and, most often, the women they violate.

Clergypeople are very susceptible to a batterer's claim of being "a changed man by God" and of deserving reconciliation. Our naiveté and lack of domestic violence training can lead us into not only pressuring a victim into forgiving her perpetrator, but also into strongly encouraging her to restore her relationship with a man who has not changed, not sought treatment, and, many times, not even shown remorse for his misdeeds.

Recall Marie's story in chapter 3. Although she had obtained a temporary restraining order (TRO) against her husband, Charlie, because of his violence against her and their children, Marie's pastor, despite having full knowledge of the TRO, still advised her to meet with her husband in an effort to restore their marriage. The results were tragic: Charlie verbally attacked his wife at that meeting and, subsequently, continued to violate her emotionally, physically, and sexually. "Forgiving does not necessarily mean automatically trusting or returning to the offender," writes Rev. Dr. Marie Fortune, a pioneer in the domestic violence movement. "Trust that has been so savagely broken can be regained only over time, if at all. The return to a relationship is entirely dependent on trust: can the survivor genuinely trust this person not to abuse her again? The choice to forgive should not be tied to these decisions."[15]

Forgiveness as Forgetting
The old folk adage "Forgive and forget" has unfortunately been quoted time and again by clergypeople and others to victims of domestic violence. The saying has brought added consternation to victims struggling with forgiveness. "Linking forgiveness with forgetting is both disturbing and inappropriate," insists Rev. Dr. Laura Delaplain, an ordained minister in the United Methodist Church and a licensed psychologist. She counsels victims of both childhood and domestic violence, and has been the director of the Norma Kent Pastoral Counseling Center in Abington, Massachusetts, for more than thirteen years. "I've personally heard a clergyperson say to a victim of domestic violence that to forgive means to forget," recalled Dr. Delaplain. "This kind of teaching can be very damaging because someone who's been victimized doesn't

need to forget the abuse. It's functional for her to remember, to help her learn from the past."

Fritz Fritschel discussed the process of how we let go of hurtful events in our lives, but not the memories of those events. "Forgiveness is not forgetting," he insisted. "Instead, it's a matter of integrating the pain associated with our hurts into a larger sense of wholeness. We never forget the past, and we don't change it either. But rather than allowing past hurts to sabotage us with bitterness and vengeance, we look for ways to let go of the rancor, to clothe it with a sense of understanding."

Everett Worthington, Jr. offered a scientific perspective on the idea of forgetting past hurts. "It's impossible to forget the past and it should be," he said. "We're hard wired to remember situations and times we've been hurt, especially situations like domestic violence." Dr. Worthington pointed out that victims sometimes misjudge the memory of an abusive episode as some kind of indication of unforgiveness. "What happens, of course, is that a victim will forgive her perpetrator, but, when she remembers some aspect of the abuse again, she'll invalidate her forgiveness. She'll say, 'Well, gee, I shouldn't be remembering this. It must mean I didn't really forgive my abuser.' One of the things we do in our program is try to help people who want to forgive to understand that it's natural to recall the hurt. It's not unforgiveness just because they remember." Worthington said it's only when we get into what he calls the "cold emotions of unforgiveness: bitterness, hostility, resentment, retaliation," that we are truly being unforgiving.

Let's go back to Cynthia's story. In 1991, after living with her abusive husband, Bob, for sixteen years, she decided to divorce him when she learned he'd been involved in a long-term affair. Cynthia admits that forgiving Bob was a process that took years. "I wanted to hang onto my anger and rage, and to see Bob punished because of all the hurt he'd caused me and our daughter," she confessed. "But I'd been around other women who had been abused and betrayed by their husbands. And the women who chose to work on the process of forgiveness seemed to be doing a lot better than those women who held grudges and sought retribution. So I decided to work on forgiveness—not for Bob's sake, but for my own health and healing."

Making the conscious effort to let go of her anger, hurt and other feelings caused by her husband's actions and behavior, Cynthia says she initially felt guilty when she remembered any aspect of Bob's abuse. "In my church denomination, forgiveness meant forgetting," she disclosed. "So I told myself I had to be nice to my ex-husband, even though he took no responsibility for all the hurt he caused me and our daughter, and he continued to blame me for his actions. I also reasoned that I had to pretend as though I'd totally forgotten the past. But now I see the concept of 'forgive and forget' as both harmful to victims and also as ridiculous. I'd have to be brainless to not remember all the evil things Bob did to me."

Nine years after her marriage ended, Cynthia now has a new view of what forgiveness is and what it is not. "It took me many years to come to the conclusion that forgiveness has nothing to do with forgetting," she said definitively. "Instead, it involves giving up the wish to punish or get even with your wrongdoer. I have let go of those thoughts and wishes regarding Bob. But I haven't forgotten all the damage he caused me and our daughter, and I never will." While she claims no longer to hate her former husband, or want to see him suffer, Cynthia also clearly has no desire to have a relationship with him. "Bob is not a nice or trustworthy person," she said. "I choose no longer to subject myself to his abuse, lies, manipulation, and his lack of accountability. Bob is a very deceptive and manipulative man and I thank God for helping me get free from him." Cynthia says she also thanks God for being able to remember the past. "My memories help me measure just how far I've come on my healing journey," she concluded. "Remembering the past also acts as an early warning system whenever I encounter abusive and violent men."

Forgiveness as Accepting Abuse

As mentioned in chapter 1, the 158 clergypeople I interviewed (and a number of other ministers I spoke with who declined to take part in this project) condemned domestic violence. The abuse of women by intimate or former intimate partners is not justifiable, everyone agreed. "Of course domestic violence is wrong," was the most common response I received from ministers when I asked them if they would describe abuse as sin. Some clergy members went so far as to say that any man who batters his wife or girlfriend in any way is not "a man of God." And yet several of these same clergypeople, and many other ministers serving in institutions, parishes, pastoral counseling centers, and social service agencies throughout the world, unwittingly contribute to the struggles victims face when it comes to the question of forgiveness.

A recent encounter with a pastoral colleague—let's call him David—will help clarify my point. The senior minister at one of Oahu's most thriving parishes, David is respected throughout the community because of the emphasis he places on equality and justice for all humankind. He is a man of character and integrity. David sought my consultation after learning from one of his parishioners, Fran, that she had been constantly victimized by her husband the entire ten years of their marriage. Complicating matters for the pastor was the fact that her husband, Alan, was also a faithful member of David's church. "I told Fran domestic violence is not of God and that it's sinful for Alan to be abusing her," announced Pastor David during a meeting in my office the day after he learned of the abuse. "But I also encouraged Fran to think about forgiving Alan as soon as possible. If she could somehow find it in her heart to put the abuse out of her mind, I said, in order to reconcile matters with Alan, then she could save the marriage and everything would be OK."

The above scenario reveals a number of all-too-common miscalculations on the part of well-intentioned clergypeople trying to provide effective and practical spiritual care to victims of domestic violence. These miscalculations lead victims to believe that ministers are rushing the forgiveness and minimizing the abuse. Let's take a closer look at how this equation gets perpetuated:

• *Encouraging a quick restoration of the marriage.* It bears repeating: forgiveness is not the same as reconciliation. Therefore, even if a victim chooses to let go of the anger, bitterness, and other feelings resulting from her partner's brutality, clergypeople must not encourage or pressure the victim into a quick reconciliation. In fact, we should strongly discourage a victim from returning to a dangerous and unhealthy situation with a partner who needs both treatment and spiritual counseling. Marie Fortune comments: "From the offender's perspective, forgiveness is often viewed as an immediate way to be relieved of guilt for wrongful actions. An offender may approach a pastor seeking forgiveness or may ask the victim to forgive. Usually these requests are accompanied by genuine remorse and promises of changed behavior: 'I'm sorry, honey, I'll never hit you again.' Or the offender may bargain with the victim: 'If you forgive me and take me back, then I'll go into treatment.' But forgiveness by the victim or by the church is inappropriate and premature in these situations. Forgiveness before justice is 'cheap grace' and cannot contribute to authentic healing and restoration to wholeness for the victim or for the offender. It cuts the healing process short and may well perpetuate the cycle of abuse. It also undercuts the redemption of abusers by preventing them from being accountable for their abusive behavior."[16]

• *Failing to discuss with a victim her understanding of forgiveness.* In the above scenario with my colleague on Oahu, David may have given more helpful pastoral care to Fran had he asked her what she understood forgiveness to mean. Many victims, especially those associated with religious faiths such as Christianity, were taught that forgiveness is the same as reconciliation, forgetting, and acting as though what happened was not that bad; that things are now OK. If, however, ministers explore with victims their understanding of forgiveness, they could help victims develop a clearer picture of what the concept is—and what it is not. "The role and meaning of forgiveness is often misinterpreted by clergy, batterers, and even by victims themselves," asserted Mimi Lind, a clinical social worker and the coordinator of the domestic violence program at the Venice Family Clinic in Venice, California. Lind says that the victims she counsels, most of them Catholic Latinas, often treat forgiveness as a remedy for the abuse they've suffered from husbands and boyfriends. "I tell battered women that just because they've decided to forgive their abusive partners doesn't mean everything will suddenly be OK," she stated. "Forgiveness is not a cure for abuse. Batterers still need to take responsibility for their actions—and need to seek treatment.

It's very common for men to use the idea of forgiveness as a weapon against their partners, or as part of the apologies that follow a violent episode. If abusive men will get help, and treat their partners with respect and empathy, then forgiveness can possibly play a role in healing a broken relationship."

The Rev. Nelda Rhoades Clarke, an ordained minister in the Church of the Brethren, is the executive director of the Emma Norton Residence, a national mission of the United Methodist Church, in St. Paul, Minnesota. Most of the women she serves are either homeless or at risk of being homeless. Nearly 100 percent of these women suffered abuse as a child or from an intimate partner as an adult, or both. The women often seek spiritual counsel from clergy regarding the matter of forgiveness. "When women come to me saying they have to forgive their abusive partner, I always ask them what they think forgiveness means," Clarke said. "Often, I have to work with these women on redefining forgiveness because many of them say their pastors told them that forgiveness means acting as though the abuse never happened, or saying everything is now OK." Clarke is deeply disturbed by these misconceptions. "Domestic violence is never OK and forgiveness doesn't at all mean forgetting," she insisted. "Clergy members must never force or encourage victims into saying or thinking abuse is either OK or needs to be forgotten in order for these victims to feel as though they are practicing forgiveness."

• *Putting the sanctity of marriage ahead of the safety of victims.* We discussed this issue in other chapters and will address it again later in this chapter. When ministers emphasize the sacred qualities of marriage (and the idea of "saving" the marriage certainly indicates just how sacred marriage is viewed by most ministers), and don't emphasize more strongly the sacred qualities of the victim, they are essentially telling abused women that their safety is less important than their marriages. Thus, many battered women get the idea that they must stay in dangerous and unhealthy relationships and also have to pretend that all is forgiven, forgotten, and OK—even though their abusive husbands have not changed in the least. "I had to forgive my husband and we had to get back together to save the marriage," Mary heard her pastors tell her even though Edward took no responsibility for his brutality against her. "They said 'forgiveness will make everything OK,' even after I told the pastors that Edward had threatened to kill both me and my children. Their bad advice put me and my kids in grave danger."

• *Not confronting the perpetrator.* Throughout his hour-long visit in my office, Pastor David never once mentioned his pastoral responsibility toward Fran's abusive husband. When I asked the minister how he planned to deal with Alan, he replied, "If Fran decides to forgive him, then everything will be OK." It's this notion that has caused many victims of domestic violence to think clergypeople equate forgiveness with saying abuse is OK. Whether or not a victim chooses to forgive her batterer, we ministers have the responsibility to confront perpetrators about the sinful nature of their actions, and to encourage them to get professional help. (Remember, as discussed in chapter 4, never confront a perpetrator without first discussing with the victim both the benefits and potential risks that such a confrontation could bring. Also, make sure the victim has a safety plan, similar to the one discussed in chapter 2, that can be implemented quickly should her husband's or boyfriend's abuse continue or escalate.) Not confronting a perpetrator can indicate to a victim that we are either blaming her for the abuse or making her responsible for her partner's damaging behavior, or both.

How Ministers Can Help Survivors Struggling with Forgiveness

Ministers can provide invaluable support to survivors struggling with the thorny question of forgiveness. Warm and sensitive responses on our part can be of great comfort to abused women as they trudge the often long and difficult road leading to spiritual and psychological renewal. We can also assist survivors who are striving to attain rejuvenated trust, both in themselves and in others.

Therefore, it is vital that our pastoral care is appropriate, effective and practical. To that end, here are some guidelines.

Be long on listening and short on advice. As was discussed in the preceding section, well-intentioned clergypeople and congregants often equate forgiveness with reconciliation, forgetting, and acting as though the abuse either was not so bad or is OK. As a result of these misconceived equations, survivors often end up enduring added pain. Recall Mary's story. Her pastors and other parishioners repeatedly told her that she had to forgive and forget all the violence Edward had perpetrated, and to reconcile with him, even though he remained irresponsible and unrepentant. The poor advice left Mary racked with guilt. "I was in such a dilemma—unable or unwilling to forgive my abusive spouse and feeling like a terrible Christian as a result," confessed Mary. "Eventually I left that parish and, for a long time, felt like I couldn't go to any other church or even turn to God for help, because I was a bad person who refused to forgive her husband."

What Mary found helpful were the times her friends spent listening to her struggles rather than offering advice. "I was able to share with a few people without feeling judged or pressured by them in any way," Mary said. "This allowed me, over a long period of time, to learn for myself the true meaning of forgiveness. I discovered it has nothing to do with forgetting, reconciling, or pretending that the abuse is OK." The most helpful spoken responses the friends gave were brief but affirming. "They might say, 'You will never forget what your ex-husband did to you, Mary, and you don't want to forget.' They'd also say, 'I'm sorry over what Edward did to you. No one deserves to suffer the abuse you suffered.' I found these words, and especially my friends' willingness to listen, very comforting."

By listening more and talking less, ministers and other people of faith provide survivors with a supportive spiritual presence and minimize the temptation to blurt out well-meant but trite advice. In chapter 2 we discussed the myriad platitudes offered to survivors by clergy members and others. We are all too quick to recite an additional set of empty ruminations about forgiveness. These sentiments keep battered women trapped in dangerous and unhealthy relationships with abusive men. When they are mixed with

Scripture—usually out of context—survivors report feeling even more guilty for falling short of these alleged "biblical truths." Therefore, clergy members and all other Christians must never make the following statements to survivors:

- Jesus tells us in the Gospel of Matthew, "If someone strikes you on the right cheek, turn to him the other also."
- Forgive and forget.
- Remember the Bible says, "If you forgive men when they sin against you, your heavenly Father will also forgive you. But if you do not forgive men their sins, your Father will not forgive your sins."
- Jesus says we are to forgive others "seventy times seven."
- If you don't forgive your husband, then it's an indication that you're not practicing Christian love.
- The Bible says, "All have sin and fallen short of the glory of God." Your husband sinned, but so have you. You must forgive him.
- To err is human, to forgive divine.
- In the book of Jeremiah we are reminded what the Lord promises: "For I will forgive their wickedness and will remember their sins no more." Follow the Lord's example and forgive your husband.
- Jesus warns, "Do not judge, or you too will be judged."
- Only those without sin, says the Lord, should cast stones at others.

Don't pressure a survivor into forgiving. Survivors must be given time to work on the process of forgiveness without any pressure from others. This may include supporting a survivor's decision to not forgive for the time being. "It puts a lot of pressure on a survivor to be told by clergy members and others that she needs to feel differently than she's feeling," according to Laura Delaplain. "When a client who's been abused tells me she's not ready to forgive her offender, that she still feels angry, resentful, and bitter toward him because of the way he has treated her, I avoid trying to change her feelings." Instead, Delaplain assures survivors that God is with them. "I tell my clients God understands their feelings and struggles, and that God can forgive—even when we're unable to. Many survivors have told me they find it healing to know they don't have to forgive on someone else's time schedule."

Two themes consistently emerged from the interviews of ministers for this book: the importance of "saving" marriages and the temptation toward quick-fix solutions. These reveal why so many clergypeople feel the need to rush survivors into forgiving an abusive spouse. Both play a critical role in keeping battered women in dangerous marriages.

The Need to Save a Marriage

"A marriage must be saved at all costs," ministers throughout the country repeatedly told me. Ironically, when I asked these same Catholic and Protestant spiritual leaders if they thought keeping a marriage together was more important than keeping a woman and her children safe from abuse, most responded, "Of course not!" One minister, a Catholic priest serving in California, expressed indignation at even being asked the question. "A pastor or anyone else would have to be an absolute sadist to even suggest that marriage is more important than the safety of women and children," the priest stated angrily. I pointed out that he himself had just told me he practiced the "save the marriage at all costs" model. That phrase implies that marriage is more important than even the safety of women and children. The priest accused me of attempting to "twist" his words with "slick psychobabble." He abruptly hung up the telephone. Ministers beware: if we say that marriages must be saved at all costs, then we are suggesting that a marriage is more important than a woman's safety! Are we ready to take responsibility for the added abuse, and maybe even death, of women and children as a result of our need for them to forgive and return to dangerous relationships?

The Temptation of the Quick-Fix Solution

A clergy colleague serving on the island of Maui telephoned me. A woman in his parish had just disclosed that her husband, also an active church member, had physically and sexually abused her during their entire five-year marriage. My colleague spoke candidly with me about his feelings: "I just hate these situations!" he shouted. "Domestic violence is so awful and messy. I'm tempted to tell this woman to forgive and forget the abuse, and to get on with her marriage. But I know enough about violence in the home to realize this kind of pastoral advice would solve nothing. It would probably make matters worse for the victim."

I appreciate my colleague's candor, and especially his insights that dissuaded him from telling his battered parishioner to forgive and forget. In truth, domestic violence is an awful, messy issue. Quick-fix solutions, however, do nothing but make matters worse for victimized women.

Still, many clergypeople express a longing to have life wrapped up in a nice, neat package. The less conflict, the better. As a result, we either minimize or totally deny such conflicts as domestic abuse among our parishioners. We may also offer highly simplified and rosy solutions to complicated matters. "Let's face it, the emotions that a victim is feeling—anger, bitterness, frustration, powerlessness, and so forth—are not emotions that any of us want to sit with for very long," noted Rev. Dr. Anne Marie Hunter, an ordained United Methodist minister. She cautions us not to pressure or rush survivors into forgiving. "I think we clergy often want to see forgiveness take place quickly, so we try to hasten survivors into meeting our need. But a survivor's process should not be hastened in any way. It needs to happen organically, without any outside pressure."

We pastors need to face the fact that our congregations are not made up of perpetually happy-go-lucky parishioners who live lives wrapped in a nice and neat package, free from conflict. Despite our desires for this type of fairy tale existence, we have to realize that both victims and perpetrators of domestic violence worship in our midst every Sunday. This "awful and messy" situation, as my Maui colleague identifies it, won't dissipate by pressuring or rushing survivors into forgiving and forgetting the abuse, or by encouraging them to restore marriages that have been damaged or destroyed by violent men. If clergy members are to provide truly effective and practical spiritual care to both victims and perpetrators, then we need to leave the comfort of our fantasy world and step into the harsh reality that survivors face daily.

Conclusion

Forgiveness is a very important aspect of wholeness and well-being. But it is not magic, not a wand waved across the landscape of our hearts, minds, and souls that will make our hurts disappear. It is not forgetting, or pretending that the wrongful acts are OK. Nor is forgiveness a promise to restore a relationship with our offender(s). Instead, forgiveness is the process of letting go, or putting aside, our right to be angry, bitter, and so forth, for having been hurt by another human being.

Forgiveness is an especially complicated issue for survivors of domestic violence, particularly if they've been raised in a religious faith such as Christianity. Having been taught by pastors, other Christians, and family and friends that forgiveness is a virtuous act necessary to keep them in harmony with God, Jesus, other people, and themselves, many survivors feel both guilty and ashamed when they are unable or unwilling immediately to forgive their transgressors.

Many clergypeople have hindered victims of domestic violence as they struggle with this issue. Our misinterpretation of the concept of forgiveness, misquoting of the Christian Scriptures, and failure to hold abusive men accountable for their violence have left survivors feeling agonized, confused, and unloved. Further, our wish to "save" marriages at all costs and our attraction to the quick-fix solution have led us to pressure abused women to forgive and return to husbands who are not repentant, have not sought (or remained in) treatment, and have taken no responsibility for all the hurt they have caused.

If clergy and other pastoral workers truly want to help survivors who are struggling with the thorny question of forgiveness, we must first commit ourselves to learning what the concept is and what it is not. Second, we must learn the accurate historical context of forgiveness in the Christian Scriptures. And third, we must demonstrate our love and concern for survivors not only by being present to their needs, but also by allowing them to work on this complicated issue in their own time frame, free from pressure from us.

Questions for Discussion

1. How do you define forgiveness? Has reading this chapter altered your definition in any way? If so, tell how.

2. Name and discuss the three concepts that are often equated with forgiveness. How are these concepts similar to and different from forgiveness? What negative impact do these common but inaccurate equations have upon survivors of domestic violence?

3. Discuss the various meanings of forgiveness in the New Testament. What were the cultural-anthropological views of the first-century Mediterranean world and how did these views influence the concept of forgiveness in the New Testament? When was interpersonal forgiveness possible and when was it not? How have New Testament passages about forgiveness been used to support survivors, and when have these caused survivors further harm? Discuss the various meanings of the Greek words *aphiēmi, charizomai,* and *apoluō*.

4. How did you react to Cynthia's story? How would you care for her, particularly during the time she was struggling with the question of forgiveness? What do you see as your role in dealing with her abusive husband, Bob? Are there any special approaches you would take because Bob is a Christian minister?

5. Discuss the dangers to a victim and her children when she is told to stay with her abusive husband to "save" her marriage. What are your feelings about the statement made by many ministers to survivors instructing them to stay in their marriages "at all costs"?

6. Do you feel qualified to provide effective and practical spiritual care to survivors struggling with the thorny question of forgiveness? If not, what do you think you are lacking? If so, describe the training you have undergone to reach this level of competency.

Chapter 6. Minister to Minister

For me, the key to understanding the notion of violence lies in the misuse of power. It really is a power issue and, theologically, that's where I think we've gone astray. For a great length of time the whole Christian church has been operating with a sense of power that has been detrimental to females, by uplifting or upholding the patriarchal form of God's power.

    —Rev. Fritz Fritschel, Assisting Pastor of the Lutheran Church of Honolulu (Evangelical Lutheran Church in America), Honolulu, Hawaii

The findings I obtained over two years while interviewing 158 Catholic and Protestant clergy have left me both hopeful and worried. Those I interviewed serve in parishes, counseling centers, and institutions across the country, and they identify themselves as conservative, evangelical, fundamental, liberal, mainline, moderate, and progressive. They were unanimous in condemning domestic abuse and all other forms of violence against women and children. They call domestic abuse criminal, deplorable, and sinful. Some of the ministers are confronting perpetrators with their accountability for the damage they have caused. But, sadly, the vast majority of spiritual leaders could not describe any plans or programs in which they are involved to address this pervasive problem.

Moreover, lack of involvement was not limited to one group or gender. To be sure, three-quarters of the clergy I interviewed are men. But most of the women clergy I spoke with also could not describe any concrete ways they are addressing the problem. Shockingly (though it was a common response among the male clergy I interviewed), a clergywoman in California stated matter-of-factly that part of the blame for domestic violence has to be placed on the female victims. If women would approach their husbands or boyfriends "more femininely," she stated, "then men would have no cause to violate them." I had assumed that women clergy would know more than men did about domestic violence; yet, most of the women I talked with seemed to lack a clear and deep understanding of its pervasiveness.

Denial certainly prevented some of the clergypeople from taking action. Male ministers in particular often remarked that because no woman in any of the parishes they have served had ever disclosed an episode of abuse to them, they concluded that no abuse existed in those homes. None of these ministers seemed to associate the lack of disclosure with the fact that they had never broached the subject of domestic violence from the pulpit, in classrooms or counseling sessions, or during their pastoral prayers. (Not surprisingly, the clergy women and men who are actively involved in the issue all cite their initiation of the subject as a vital first step in helping a victim feel more comfortable and safe about sharing her story.)

A host of misconceptions also plague some of the clergy members. Several suggested that domestic violence is found only within certain cultural, racial, and socioeconomic groups. It doesn't exist in affluent and rural areas, or in any family where "Christ is at the center." Such beliefs, however, are inaccurate and naive; domestic violence exists everywhere!

The words of a white pastor serving a large parish in Milwaukee offended me on a personal level. Applauding what he called my "fortitude" for tackling such a difficult problem, he said it was especially important that I, an African American man, stay actively involved. "As I'm sure you already know, domestic violence is rampant among your people," instructed the pastor. "When will black men see how stupid they are for abusing their women and children?" Taken aback, I pointed out to him that African American men aren't the only perpetrators of domestic and family violence. National statistics indicate that many violent crimes that occur inside or outside the home—assaults, murders, and rapes—are perpetrated by white men and boys. This revelation did not sway the pastor's thinking. He called my data "lopsided," and then abruptly ended our interview.

Finally, fear plays a major role in preventing clergy from intervening in domestic violence situations. A pastor I interviewed who served a church in Florida said he was afraid that getting "mixed up in a private family matter" such as spousal abuse could end up costing him and his church millions of dollars in lawsuits. Most of my clergy interviewees feared saying or doing something that might cause victims more harm. I can appreciate their concern, for this is an extremely complex and difficult issue. And yet, while many of these ministers readily admitted to feeling ill-equipped, few said they were taking advantage of the many articles, books, videotapes, and workshops that address the subject. Some said they didn't have time to read these resources or get training. I don't doubt the legitimacy of this claim; most ministers are extremely busy. But how will we care effectively for abused women and children and their perpetrators if we don't set aside time to learn how to do so?

In contrast, twenty-five of the clergypeople I interviewed are actively involved in addressing the issue. They frequently preach, pray, study, teach, write, and offer consultation on domestic violence. Some have helped to establish and implement counseling and retreat centers, shelters, transition houses, and other places of healing and safety for abused women and their children. What compelled these ministers to get involved? Why do they think other spiritual leaders are reluctant to deal with the problem? How would they advise and challenge our misinformed or uninvolved colleagues?

Compelling Factors

It was something I had never anticipated or expected. No one does if they haven't been raised in an atmosphere of family violence and abuse. There was no such history in my family, and I had personally never witnessed abuse. So I thought my own family was immune.

—Rev. Robert S. Owens, Jr., Minister in the Presbyterian Church (U.S.A.) (retired)

Robert Owens confessed that he had spent the first three decades of his ministry avoiding the issue of domestic violence. "I had a very limited understanding of the problem. If someone back then would have asked me for a definition of domestic violence, I probably would not have included things like threats, acts of intimidation, harassment, or verbal abuse; nor would I have thought unmarried people could be considered vulnerable. Domestic violence meant to me a man beating his wife." But Owens said his views on the subject changed dramatically in the late 1980s. That's when he learned that his own daughter was being victimized by her husband.

"It was something I had never anticipated or expected," the minister said. "No one does if they haven't been raised in an atmosphere of family violence and abuse. There was no such history in my family, and I had personally never witnessed abuse. So I thought my own family was immune." The pastor's daughter had no idea that her husband had a history of abusive and violent behavior. He'd presented himself as both charming and kind during their period of dating. "As most men do, he extended only his good side to my daughter during courtship," the pastor recalled. "He came across as being very gentle, tender, and loving." A short time into the marriage, however, Owens's daughter began to realize that her husband had some serious problems. "His intimidation of my daughter started almost immediately," Owens said, "as did his accusations that she was being an unfaithful wife. He was an insanely jealous man."

Initially, Pastor Owens knew nothing about the abuse. "Like most women, our daughter hid her husband's behavior from us," he said. "Many abused women are embarrassed, ashamed, fearful, and, for many reasons, they don't share their concerns with those who love them most. But finally our daughter called from the state where she and this man were living at the time and told us there was a problem. We suggested she come home and stay a while with us, which she did. At the same time, we encouraged her husband to get some professional help. He also took our advice, and they lived with us." But the abuse recurred and eventually escalated. The minister ordered his son-in-law to leave their home. One night the man returned, uninvited. "My wife was out of town at the time," Owens said, "and my daughter and I had been out with friends all day. On the way home I stopped off for groceries while my daughter went on to the house. Her husband had broken in and was waiting for her. He had pulled the phone cords out of the wall so she could not call out. When my daughter entered the house, her husband attacked her."

Having attempted to defend his daughter from her husband during past abusive episodes, Owens also became a target of his son-in-law's violence. When he arrived home from the grocery store he too was attacked. "My daughter screamed, 'Dad, he has a knife!' The next thing I knew, her husband was attacking me in the hallway and saying he was going to kill me. Somehow, I managed to take the knife from him, and he fled. I thought I'd lost an eye, which was very traumatic for me." It took forty stitches to repair the pastor's eye, and Owens's daughter needed medical attention as well for a stab wound and other bruises. Both victims eventually recovered fully from the physical aspects of the assault. "This experience of violence in our own family ultimately led me to become personally involved in the issue of domestic violence," Owens acknowledged.

The church Owens was pastoring at the time he and his daughter were attacked was very supportive. Members of the congregation also became actively involved in the issue of domestic violence, leasing a residence and, ultimately, opening a transition house for abused women and their children. In addition, the church began sponsoring an annual prayer vigil for the families of victims who die from domestic violence. Owens began addressing the issue in sermons and corporate prayer. The response was dramatic. "Victims started making appointments with me almost immediately," he said. "And they never stopped coming." It was when the pastor began addressing the issue from the pulpit and in his intercessory prayer that women felt they could risk sharing their secret with him. "I had to show victims some pastoral concern first before they felt they could trust me. I think that's always true—any church is going to take on the lifestyle of its leadership. When I, as leader, started addressing domestic violence openly, then victims and members of the entire congregation began to know that it was a problem they could safely discuss."

"That was really a transforming moment for me, because I was awed by these women who were courageous enough to tell their stories in order to make a point. And they were willing to ask me, a male pastor no less, to address a significant societal issue in a very positive and helpful way."

—REV. DR. RODNEY E. WILMOTH, PASTOR OF THE HENNEPIN AVENUE UNITED METHODIST CHURCH, MINNEAPOLIS, MINNESOTA

Rodney Wilmoth had been involved with the issue of domestic violence for more than fifteen years by the time he became senior pastor of Hennepin Avenue United Methodist Church, a large, affluent parish near downtown Minneapolis. One day four women from the church asked for an appointment with him. "One of the women was a staff member," remembered Wilmoth. "She said that she and three other women in the congregation wanted to visit with me on a personal item. I hadn't been at the church very long, so I had no idea what they wanted to see me about."

On the day of their meeting, the women told Wilmoth they had two reasons they'd come to see him. First, they wanted to share their stories of childhood and adult abuse. Second, the women wanted to inform their pastor that they were only four of many victims in the congregation. "Apparently, they felt my office was a safe environment and that I would listen to them," said Wilmoth. They each told him a heart-wrenching story. Two women had been repeatedly sexually abused as a child, one by her father, the other by another male figure in the family. The third woman talked about being raped at a young age, which resulted in her subsequently becoming involved in a series of unhealthy relationships with men. And the fourth woman described incidents of emotional and physical abuse perpetrated by a lover.

After telling their stories, the women gave a third reason for their visit. They wanted the pastor to consider addressing the issue of violence against women and children in his sermons. "The women weren't asking me to necessarily devote an entire sermon to abuse," he insisted. "But they did ask me to at least call attention to some of the statistics about childhood and domestic abuse."

Wilmoth began including the subjects of abuse and violence in his Sunday morning sermons. "It wasn't so much a matter of my citing statistics," the pastor explained. "It was a matter of me, as a minister, saying from the pulpit, for example, 'If one in every four women are sexually abused as children, then surely there are women in the congregation this morning who've been abused sexually as a child. Many of these women have had to grow up with the feeling that the abuse was their fault.'" According to Wilmoth, the response has always been very affirming. "When I talk about people being victimized and I acknowledge that victims aren't only outside our church but also worshiping among us, members of the congregation always come up to me afterward and say, 'Thank you so much for saying that.'"

Rodney Wilmoth traces his enlightenment directly to the four women's disclosures. "That was really a transforming moment for me, because I was awed by these women who were courageous enough to tell their stories in order to make a point. And they were willing to ask me, a male pastor no less, to address a significant societal issue in a very positive and helpful way. I think if all ministers had the opportunity I did with the four women, then they'd also experience a wake-up call. We may be more enlightened today and have statistics at our fingertips. But the fact of the matter is, were it not for those women I might still be plodding along in the dark."

> "Part of my journey now is to answer the questions, What do and don't I want to pass along to my daughter? What's been helpful and unhelpful in my own upbringing and faith journey? I don't want to pass along to her a judging male God. And I don't want my daughter to grow up with a God that can't look like her. How we think about God affects our attitudes and behavior."

—Rev. Julie Mall, Minister in the Presbyterian Church (U.S.A.), Minneapolis, Minnesota

Growing up in the 1960s, Julie Mall learned the images of God that prevailed in those times and that continue today. "God was male, a father, an old man with stern eyes and a beard. God was a distant figure pointing a judging finger," recalls the former hospital and prison chaplain. "My church didn't invite me to examine, ponder, question, or wonder beyond these images. Therefore, I grew up believing that since God didn't look like me, I wasn't created in God's image. I got the message that I was somehow inferior because I was female." But when Mall began seminary in the early 1980s, her theological perspective started to change. "On closer examination of the Scriptures I began to question some of the things I thought were true, things I once held dear. I discovered there were different ways to look at biblical texts."

Delving into the Hebrew and Greek manuscripts of the Old Testament, Mall began to experience God in ways she never had before. "It was a very empowering period of time for me," she recalled. "I started to discover the number of scriptural passages that affirm the equality of men and women. The first creation story in Genesis, for instance, portrays a God that created humankind, female and male, in God's image. Why is this version not well known?"

Mall found the same egalitarian theme in the Christian Scriptures. "Jesus totally overturned the mores of his society," she pointed out. "He challenged the perception that women were unclean and were the property of men. They weren't supposed to talk to or touch a man in public. But Jesus welcomed women into his inner circle of followers. He taught, healed, ate with, and spoke with women. He let women care for him. He let women touch him, and clean his feet with their hair. His close women followers stayed with him while he was dying on the cross. After he died, it was those women who first experienced and proclaimed that Jesus was still with them. Even in the letters that Paul wrote there is a strong sense of equality and mutuality between the sexes within the early Christian communities. Paul even talks about women in the roles of leader, teacher, deacon, apostle, missionary, and patron. Why do we not often hear about that? And these are the same texts that people use most often to justify or excuse abuse, domination, and exclusion of women or to blame women for their own victimization."

After her daughter was born in 1990, Julie Mall became even more fervent about addressing the moral and social systems that continue to keep females in a state of oppression. "I didn't want my daughter to grow up like I did, thinking she's inferior to males and that God views her less favorably because she is female," she said emphatically. "So, after her birth, I began looking even closer at the messages about females and males both in Christianity and throughout the rest of the world." Mall became particularly aware of what churches were teaching about traditions and the Bible. Some of these teachings contribute to oppression and injustice, including child and domestic abuse. "Promoting an authoritarian male image of God can help keep females in an inferior position," Mall contended. "Most of the major world religions are still based on images of a God or gods that are male. The Bible and other holy books were written by men, translated by men, and primarily interpreted by men. Religion and scriptures both have been used to justify domination, rape, murder, and many other forms of abuse and injustice that continue to be perpetrated against females around the world. Promoting an image of God as male—which is only one of an endless list of metaphors used in the Bible to describe God, but which is the only one many people accept—makes it easier for males to claim superiority over females. How we think about God affects our attitudes and behavior."

Determined to teach her daughter a more egalitarian view than she herself was raised on, Mall feels both challenged and inspired. "Part of my journey now is to answer the questions, What do and don't I want to pass along to my daughter? What's been helpful and unhelpful in my own upbringing and faith journey? I don't want to pass along to her a judging male God. And I don't want my daughter to grow up with a God that can't look like her. I want to pass along the idea that God can be like many different things. God can be male, female, a butterfly, or light. God can be a mother hen or anything else my daughter wishes to imagine that is helpful and empowering for her. I want my daughter to see a God that can look like her, and I want her to feel as though she can look like God. I want her to know that God is within and around her. Also, I want her to grow up full of life and courage and having good feelings about being born a female." Mall is clear about one other issue: her role in helping her daughter to accomplish these goals. "I realized shortly after she was born that I needed to show my daughter books and tell her stories with many images of God," she concluded. "And I knew also, both as a mother and as a clergyperson, that I had to speak and write about the many forms of injustice and oppression that both the church and society continue to promote and excuse."

"Domestic violence is a closeted issue. Much of the abuse remains either in the dark or it's hidden, often times even within the walls of our churches. Take, for instance, my stepfather. He was a 'weekender': drinking, gambling, womanizing, and abusing my mother on Fridays and Saturdays. But, on Sundays, he'd often be sober enough to attend morning worship. He was even an officer of the church. Like I said, it's in the closet. So ministers must be properly trained in order to help bring the problem out into the light."

—Rev. Clarence G. Robinson, Pastor of St. Mark African Methodist Episcopal Church, Milwaukee, Wisconsin

Clarence Robinson's mother remarried when he was five years old. He describes his stepfather as a "weekender." "He'd bring his paycheck home on Fridays and would immediately give it to my mother, asking only for ten dollars for himself," recalls the minister. But around midnight the stepfather would return home drunk, demanding that his wife give him more money. "There were times when Mother would refuse his request," Robinson said. "That's when the abuse would start." Almost every weekend as a young boy, Clarence Robinson helplessly witnessed his mother being victimized. "My stepfather was a big man, six-foot-two. He was also a street fighter. He'd curse my mother out, beat her at times, and would then usually take all the money for the week, drinking and gambling it away. I developed a habit of covering my head with a pillow, trying desperately to drown out the sounds of his brutality."

After being diagnosed with having a cancerous brain tumor, Robinson's stepfather abused his wife all the more. "One of the things he'd love to do was fuss. We couldn't tell what was going to set him off: the way my mother arranged the furniture, the alcohol he consumed, losing a bet, or if he had a bad time with one of his many girlfriends. In addition to being a drunk and a gambler, my stepfather was also a womanizer. He truly had a Jekyll-and-Hyde personality. He could be a nice fellow at times. On the other hand, he could be really mean."

At age seventeen, Clarence Robinson confronted his stepfather one weekend night. "As usual he came home drunk, asking my mother for more money," he recalled. "Mother must have refused his request because, from my bedroom, I heard him yell at her, 'Give me all my damn money!' Next thing I knew, my mother came running into my room and she crawled underneath the bed. I got up and went into the room where my stepfather was. 'That's the last time you're ever gonna mess with my mother,' I told him. I don't know what I would have done had he challenged me or hurt Mother again, but I certainly meant what I said. I'd had enough of him abusing her."

Determined not to repeat the violence he witnessed for twelve years as a child, Clarence Robinson made a commitment to God and himself as a young man. "I promised myself never to mistreat my spouse or kids, never to gamble, and never to partake of alcohol or anything else that would put me in a different state of mind," the minister said. "Many of the guys I grew up around became abusers and alcoholics, so I know the potential was there for me to do the same. I thank God for helping me to avoid these things." Robinson made another commitment as a young man: he answered God's call to the ministry. In the past twenty years Robinson has attended several classes and workshops and read many books on domestic abuse. He also frequently mentions this concern in his pastoral prayers and, on occasion, has preached entire sermons on domestic violence. The pastor offers spiritual care to abused women, and he confronts perpetrators, especially churchgoing men who claim biblical justification for their actions. "I think confronting men who abuse, particularly those men who are members of our congregations, is definitely a part of a pastor's role," Robinson insisted. "Why perpetuate the problem by looking the other way? We must try to get abusers the help they need, challenging them to join a batterers' group or to seek counseling. We can't help them if we ignore the problem—like so many ministers unfortunately do."

Looking back on his youth, Robinson is all the more determined to continue to address the violence that women, like his own mother, have had to endure for centuries. "Domestic violence is a closeted issue," he concluded. "Much of the abuse remains either in the dark or it's hidden, often times even within the walls of our churches. So ministers must be properly trained in order to help bring the problem out into the light."

"The experiences I've had, including those related to domestic abuse, have made me a stronger person. I like where I am now. I could never have said that even five years ago. These experiences have brought a depth to my life that I now really appreciate."

—Rev. Joan Ishibashi, Minister in the United Church of Christ; Associate Conference Minister for Administration and Resources, Honolulu, Hawaii

For more than a decade, Joan Ishibashi repressed memories of the physical, psychological, and sexual abuse she suffered from a man she dated for two years while attending college. "I worked hard at trying to keep that relationship out of my consciousness," the minister said. "After college I met a really kind and considerate man I ended up marrying. I earned a Master of Divinity degree from Princeton Theological Seminary, went through a divorce, and was then involved in a three-year relationship with another man who had a very violent temper. But none of these events triggered memories of the abuse from my college days."

In the late 1980s, Ishibashi and several of her friends and colleagues living in Hawaii attended a series of workshops on domestic violence facilitated by noted expert Marie Fortune. Receiving a grant shortly thereafter from a local church, the group asked Ishibashi to consider becoming the executive director of the organization they named Interfaith Network Against Domestic Violence. The group visited churches across the state, giving lectures, sermons, and workshops on domestic abuse. In addition, they provided educational opportunities for clergy. Eventually, they began a support group for abused women. "Initially, I decided to accept the invitation to become executive director of the agency not because I was so involved in dealing with domestic violence, but because I needed a job," Ishibashi confessed. "However, I also had the strong sense that I needed to be a part of this social justice issue. So when the position was offered I took it."

While she received training, Ishibashi suddenly found herself beginning to remember her past. "As I read more of the material and involved myself in a number of the workshops, memories of my own abuse came back," disclosed the minister. "For all those years I hadn't seen myself as a victim. I had thought that what I'd gone through in college, the emotional, physical, and sexual abuse, was because I deserved it, just as my boyfriend had always said. Like so many other women, I blamed myself for his abusive and violent behavior."

Ishibashi can recall one particular two-day training session that helped her realize she had in fact been victimized. "The facilitators asked us a series of questions about our relationship with intimate partners. Had any of us ever been hit, kicked, raped, or been told we were unattractive, stupid, etc.? On all these questions, and so many more, I had to answer yes. At the end of the two-day training I was drained, about to burst into tears."

From that point on, Ishibashi's commitment to work with victims of domestic violence and sexual assault grew. She began addressing these topics more frequently, and her passion for this work has never waned. "When women share their stories of abuse with me I can sense an immediate bond between us," Ishibashi said. "After that intense two-day workshop, I began to realize my story was not unlike theirs. Maybe it's not as dramatic as the ones involving frequent broken bones or hospitalizations, but there is still a deep connection. That's why I feel so committed to continue doing this work."

Why Aren't More Clergypeople Involved?

I think clergy must make it better known that their church is a safe place for abused women. Somehow, we need to make ourselves more available to these women, demonstrating that we will in no way judge them or force them to do anything. We have to provide a confidential and safe environment for victims, so that they won't have to walk that long road alone.

— FATHER BOB ROONEY, PRIEST OF ST. JOSEPH'S CATHOLIC CHURCH, BROKEN BOW, NEBRASKA

The twenty-five female and male ministers I interviewed who frequently address various aspects of domestic violence identified five themes that they believe contribute to the reluctance of many clergypeople to become involved in the issue. They cite denial, fear and helplessness, lack of appropriate training, sexism, and the fact that some clergy are themselves perpetrators of domestic abuse. Let us take a closer look at each of these themes.

Denial

In her book *The Battered Wife: How Christians Confront Family Violence,* sociologist and University of New Brunswick professor Nancy Nason-Clark reveals the findings she acquired from interviewing more than one thousand evangelical clergy serving in Eastern Canada. Though cognizant of the rate of violence in the world outside the church, the ministers in her study seemed unaware of its prevalence within their own congregations.

Moreover, Nason-Clark found that spiritual leaders—conservative and liberal alike—resisted the notion that violence could occur in Christian marriages. "Regardless of the denominational stripe of the clerical participants, there is considerable resistance to the notion that religious families can be violent. Moreover, the greatest challenge I find in addressing clerical audiences is that ministers become quite agitated when evidence is presented that men of faith sometimes have a desire to control their wives, and may even use force to ensure that control. Any challenge to the 'happy family living' motif so prevalent in Christian circles stirs the ire of many. My point here is quite straightforward: in my experience, clerical audiences are distinct from either lay church or secular audiences in that they are very reluctant to question the nuclear family unit or the sacredness of family togetherness."[1]

My conversations with spiritual leaders over a two-year period revealed findings similar to those of Nason-Clark. The majority of the 158 clergypeople I interviewed (as well as several other ministers who declined to be interviewed) claimed that domestic abuse was "not an issue" in their congregations. When Christ is at the center of a household, explained one pastor, then violence is simply not "in the heart of a man."

Nelda Rhoades Clarke, a minister in the Church of the Brethren serving in St. Paul, Minnesota, has also encountered a vast amount of denial when she has spoken to Christian groups across the country. "People are surprised to learn that someone like me experienced violence at home while growing up," Clarke said. "Often they'll say, 'You don't look like an abuse victim.' We have images of what abused women look like: they're broken and we're going to see bruises all over their bodies. People have actually said to me, 'I don't see any bruises, therefore you weren't really abused.'"

Clarke is especially troubled when clergy members express this view. "Ministers tend to discount any woman who says she's been abused verbally or sexually," Clarke said. "And when a married woman suggests that she's being sexually abused by her husband, most pastors respond, 'You're married; how can that be?' The point is that ministers don't want to believe domestic violence happens in our society, let alone in our own church or community. So we try to deny or explain it away, rather than to address it."

Denial among the clergy I interviewed crossed denominational, doctrinal, and gender lines. Pastors who support the male headship/female submission model of marriage categorically denied that this model contributes to men's ill-treatment of women. Any man who misuses the "God-given authority he possesses over his wife is really not a man of God," stated a male minister serving a Milwaukee church that teaches male headship. I suggested to him that part of the problem lay in the fact that his denomination and other Christian groups tell husbands they are the head of their wives. This makes it easier, I said, for men to twist the Scriptures to support their abuse and dominance. "Clearly the Bible teaches that a man is to be the head of his household and women are to submit to their husbands," the pastor countered. "The problem isn't in male headship, but is due to the fact that, throughout the ages, mankind has misused Scripture for his own gain. For example, Scripture has been used not only to justify domestic abuse, but also slavery and many other forms of bigotry."

The female ministers I interviewed were eager to discuss how their male colleagues contribute to the problem of domestic violence by denying the prevalence of the issue, and because of male privilege and sexism. "It's about time a man stood up and joined the ranks," declared a female pastor serving in the Southern California area upon learning I was writing this book. "Male clergy have done nothing but keep women and children in dangerous situations."

I do not deny this minister's contention, nor the beliefs of several other female clergy I interviewed who suggest that not only have many male ministers been unhelpful, but their inaction has actually contributed to the violence perpetrated against women and their children. Nevertheless, as I stated at the beginning of this chapter, of the forty female ministers I interviewed for the book, the majority fail to address domestic violence. The denial I witnessed among women clergy manifested itself in another way: A number of them said that since most of the perpetrators of violence against women and children are males, it's up to male pastors and other men to "fix the problem." When I asked these women what they saw as their specific role as clergy members regarding addressing the issue of domestic violence, few offered a concrete response. One, a pastor serving two small parishes in Ohio, declared, "I don't think women clergy should have a role. This is a male issue." By remaining uninvolved because this is a "male problem," these clergywomen, I believe, are choosing to help abused women stay in a victim role.

One form of denial revealed itself solely among uninvolved ministers who identified themselves as liberals. They claimed that domestic violence is found primarily in so-called fundamentalist or conservative churches. Several advised me to "speak with the conservatives" if I wanted to talk to clergy members who were the real contributors to the problem. I strongly disagree. Although I found that conservative and fundamentalist clergypeople certainly contribute to the problem by means of one or more of the themes discussed in this section, I also discovered the same to be true with ministers from across the denominational spectrum. As Neal MacPherson—a United Church of Christ minister who serves Church of the Crossroads, one of the most liberal parishes in Hawaii—observed, "I don't think the problem lies just with fundamentalist preachers. I think that so-called liberal preachers who don't want to deal with the issue, who can't detect the signs, are also dismissing the problem of domestic violence." Rev. Patrick Handlson, pastor of the First Presbyterian Church (U.S.A.) in Hastings, Minnesota, expressed additional concerns. "The problem with liberal, social justice clergy," he said, "is that we tend to move away from Scripture and let conservatives have it. I think that's a big mistake. Instead of challenging the way conservative clergy interpret and misinterpret Scripture, we deny this important aspect of our calling and let them say whatever they want. Liberals also have to read the Hebrew and Greek and then stand up for what we believe. Instead, what we've too often done is give away our positions on domestic violence and on other issues by not relying on Scripture."

Fear and Helplessness

There's a fear on the part of many clergypeople of being put in the middle of a situation of domestic violence, especially if both the husband and wife are a part of the church community."
—Rev. Neal MacPherson, United Church of Christ Minister and Pastor of Church of the Crossroads, Honolulu, Hawaii

An article in *Leadership* tells how Pastor Seth Johnson discovered a case of domestic violence among his parishioners. Visiting a parishioner named Marge in the hospital a few days after she had undergone a hysterectomy, Pastor Johnson learned that during Marge's entire twenty-five-year marriage, her husband, Don, had been abusing her. Don forced Marge to maintain a log of all of her daily activities, made inappropriate and hurtful comments about her weight, such as calling her "hippo" and "double-butt," and told Marge she was "too stupid" to manage money. The situation was made more complicated for Pastor Seth because Don was his most trusted elder. In the eight years they had known one another, the minister had always assumed Don was a loving husband, not at all like the cruel man Marge described. On the other hand, Marge had never seemed like a liar to Pastor Johnson. Torn, the pastor wanted to drop the issue and toyed with treating the whole situation with benign neglect.[2]

Complicated circumstances like the one just described cause many clergypeople to feel fearful and helpless when they encounter a case of domestic violence. Often, both the victim and victimizer are members of the congregation, and pastors fear not only getting in the middle of a "private matter," but also feel helpless regarding how best to care for both the victim and the perpetrator.

"Most pastors feel woefully inadequate to deal with domestic violence issues," said Rev. Robert S. Owens, Jr. "I think we are afraid of being partial. We want to be impartial, and we fear showing favoritism to a husband or wife in a domestic squabble. Nowadays, of course, there is also the fear of litigation. Many pastors have been sued for either giving too much, or what has been perceived as poor or wrong advice, and they have been blamed for the divorce because they've encouraged the woman to leave an abusive marriage."

Several clergypeople discussed their overall uneasiness with conflict in general, particularly conflicts between intimate partners. "We all have arguments," said a Protestant minister in Tennessee. "How would you like it if someone stuck their nose in your private life?" Explaining the difference between the disagreements that occur in most intimate partnerships from time to time, and acts of control, intimidation, harassment, and other forms of physical, psychological, and sexual battering, did nothing to alter the pastor's way of thinking. He labeled my description of domestic abuse as "a matter of opinion," and vowed to continue to stay out of other people's "private affairs."

The description of domestic abuse as a "private" matter was a common thread woven throughout my interviews with clergypeople, especially male clergy. At the core of this prevailing notion was the feeling of fear and helplessness. "I don't know what to do or say in these situations, and fear I'll do or say something that'll cause victimized women more harm," confessed a Catholic priest serving a parish in Connecticut. Rev. Dr. Joe Boone Abbott, a Southern Baptist minister, pastoral counselor, and marriage and family therapist serving in Birmingham, Alabama, offers another reason why clergy are reluctant to become involved in the issue. "Clergy basically like to have things appear to be positive and upbeat," Dr. Abbott stated. "Domestic violence can punch a hole through these facades, forcing ministers to see life much more honestly and realistically." This sentiment was shared by Rev. Dr. Peter Fribley, a Presbyterian minister in Madison, Wisconsin. "I think we as clergy live in kind of a protected world with a lot of energy spent on putting on a good face," Dr. Fribley asserted. "We can go a long time without hearing where people really are."

When I asked how they would address a situation of domestic violence if both the victim and the perpetrator were members of their congregation, clergy used terms such as "messy," "sticky," and "troubling." Many acknowledged that they would not know what to do. Although I appreciate the honesty of their response, it leaves me deeply troubled. Not one of the clergypeople who made this statement went on to commit themselves to attending a workshop, for instance, or reading a book on the topic. Why?

Another response troubled me even more. The spiritual leaders did not say that their first order of business was to secure a victim's safety (as I advise in chapter 2). Instead, along with "saving a marriage at all costs," they gave top priority to determining which partner was "telling the truth." I cautioned that bringing the victim together with her perpetrator to somehow "get at the truth" was extremely dangerous for the woman and her children. Despite this warning, many ministers said they would continue the practice of "weeding out the liar," as a pastor in Texas called it, by bringing together victims with their perpetrators. But, as the story below illustrates, "weeding out the liar" is a complicated matter.

Lack of Appropriate Training

I had been serving in my first full-time chaplaincy position for less than a year when a twenty-one-year-old woman, Dolores, came to my office. A month earlier, thirty-three weeks pregnant, she'd given birth to her first child, a girl. Although the baby was breathing on her own, she required several weeks of hospitalization in the hospital's Neonatal Intensive Care Unit (NICU) for close observation and to establish oral feedings. I blessed Dolores's daughter shortly after she was born and, subsequently, visited Dolores and her husband, Thomas, in the NICU on a regular basis. The couple seemed always to be enjoying each other's company, frequently embracing and constantly smiling at each other. And, like most first-time parents, Dolores and Thomas doted on their daughter. The day before the baby was released from the hospital, Dolores stopped by my office, unannounced.

"Please keep Tommy and me in your prayers, Pastor Al," requested Dolores as sadness suddenly took over her normally jovial face. "I want so much to be a good wife and mother. But . . . uh . . . but . . . I, I . . . ." The young woman's words trailed off as she suddenly burst into tears. Eventually, Dolores was able to tell me how, at times, she "disappointed" Thomas. She said she wasn't very good at golf or tennis, didn't like to bike or jog, and she hadn't yet learned how to cook like Thomas's mother. As a result, Dolores disclosed, her husband often told her that although he could have married anyone he desired, he ended up settling for a "retard." Thomas also belittled her while she was pregnant, Dolores said. He told his wife that she was "as fat as a blimp and twice as stupid." His words really hurt, Dolores told me, but she claimed she deserved the verbiage for not being "a good Christian wife."

I didn't have a clue as to how to respond to Dolores. Supporting victims of domestic abuse was certainly not a topic discussed at the seminary I attended in the late 1970s, nor was it part of my training as of 1985 when the conversation with Dolores occurred. I knew, however, that if Dolores was telling the truth, Thomas's behavior was inappropriate. And, as a Christian minister, I also knew it was my responsibility to confront him. So I asked Dolores to go to the NICU (where Thomas was visiting their daughter) and bring Thomas back to my office with her. This would help me "get at the truth," or so I thought.

Returning fifteen minutes later, Dolores and Thomas entered my office embracing and smiling as usual. Despite the tender and warm scene, I still felt it was my pastoral duty to confront Thomas on what Dolores had told me. "Name calling and belittling one's wife, Thomas, is not appropriate behavior and it's a clear affront to God's instructions about marriage," I firmly stated. "You need to stop this kind of sinful behavior immediately." Looking at me with the innocence of a sleeping child, Thomas denied ever calling Dolores inappropriate names or belittling her in any other fashion. He loved his wife more than he loved himself, the young husband proclaimed. When I glanced over at Dolores, I noticed her smile had been replaced by a blank stare. Unable to determine what she was feeling or thinking, I asked Dolores whether she had anything she wanted to say. After remaining silent for several moments she softly replied, "Everything's fine, Pastor Al." Shortly thereafter the couple left my office. It was the last time I ever saw Dolores and Thomas.

I'll never know just how much more abuse Dolores had to suffer from Thomas because of my ill-conceived pastoral care approach of bringing the couple together to "get at the truth." The ignorant and poor judgment I made still haunts me to this day. Had I attended just one lecture or workshop on domestic violence, or read only one article or book on the subject, I would have known that victims seldom make up stories about abuse. If anything, they often minimize or deny the abuse out of fear, embarrassment, shame, and for a host of other reasons. And I would have known the many potential dangers for a victim and her children when they are urged to attend couple's counseling. I now know that clergypeople must get specific training in order properly to minister to victims and perpetrators. Otherwise, they will most likely end up either giving bad advice or, as I did with Dolores, offering suggestions that can potentially cause victims more harm than good.

"Some ministers who try to counsel victims don't know what they're doing," asserts Rev. Neal MacPherson. "They don't know the emotional or psychological trauma brought on by years of abuse and violence, and end up making matters worse for a victim and her children. Victims of domestic violence need someone who really understands the complex dynamics of the problem and who is trained in family systems." Dr. James D. Moebes, senior minister of Mountain Brook Baptist Church in Birmingham, Alabama, also voices concern over ministers with little or no training who attempt to counsel victims. "Clergy need to know their limitations," the pastor warns. "If they don't understand the dynamics of the situation, the emotional issues involved, and what a victim is dealing with, then they need to have those professionals to whom they can make referrals." Father Dan Smith, an ordained Episcopal priest who serves as pastor at St. Timothy's Episcopal Church in West Des Moines, Iowa, believes ministers have to remain current in their scholarship. He is often shocked when he enters the office of ministerial colleagues: "I see on the shelves plenty of books from their seminary days, but very few books since that time. We owe it to our congregations to keep doing our homework, learning new things in new areas. Issues of violence, I think, are escalating, not going away. So it's one of the areas that clergy ought to be studying."

Sexism

The religious community has a significant foot in the patriarchal structure. In the reinforcement of traditional gender roles, for example, pastors become a part of the problems associated with domestic violence.

—Rev. Dr. Anne Marie Hunter, United Methodist Minister, Founder and Executive Director of Boston Justice Ministries, Boston, Massachusetts

Would clergy and other pastoral ministers display the same apathy toward victims of domestic violence if one quarter of all adult American men were being victimized? If wives abused and battered their husbands at an epidemic rate, would clergypeople continue to speak about the sanctity of marriage and the demonizing qualities of divorce? How many male clergy would still actually preach and teach about the importance of submission if husbands were the ones being told to submit to the authority of their wives?

Sexism remains a major factor in preventing clergypeople, especially male clergy, from becoming involved in addressing the issue of domestic violence. As we saw in chapter 1, our society in both its religious and secular circles continues strongly to perpetuate male dominance by the encouragement and excusing of men's violence and the blaming of women for their own victimization. "Domestic violence is just the latest in a series of anti-male causes," raged a male pastor serving a congregation in New York State. When I asked him to elaborate on his statement he readily replied, "I don't believe any of the so-called accurate statistics that indicate there's an overabundance of violence against women. Things are no different for women today than they were, say, one hundred years ago." I told the minister that on that point we agreed: women are viewed in the same degrading manner as they've been viewed since the beginning of time. Hearing this, the pastor accused me of being "one of them," which he refused to explain further, and then told me he was "too busy" to be a part of the book.

Further, a male pastor in Texas said that the entire premise of my book was "misguided." I should not be pointing out the lack of pastoral involvement in dealing with domestic violence, he said. The issue has much more to do with "a bunch of over-emotional, man-hating females" than with males having the need to be in control and feel powerful. I should be encouraging women to "let go of their anger and be forgiving." Interestingly, Rev. Joan Ishibashi receives similar responses from males each time she speaks to clergypeople and laity about domestic abuse. "I've actually had a couple of men who were so upset over what I've said that they've stood up during my sermon and shouted out something to me," she recalled. "I can't remember exactly what they said, but one man dismissed the whole notion of abuse and said we needed to be forgiving."

Let's revisit the issue of male headship/female submission in marriage, because I believe the teachings are rooted in sexism—the desire to preserve the patriarchal structure regardless of the consequences to women (and children). Fifty-six of the male ministers I interviewed said they teach headship/submission in their parish. All of them strongly disagreed with my assertion that these doctrines contribute to the ill-treatment of women by husbands who justify abusive behavior with claims of God-given authority over their wives. Headship and submission are not the problem, I was repeatedly told by ministers who embrace these concepts. Domestic abuse is instead caused by the "sinful nature of man."

Further, proponents of these teachings said headship and submission had to be taught in order for clergy to "maintain biblical accuracy." I doubt this supposition because when I offered the ministers egalitarian renderings of the Greek words *kephale*, which in addition to "head" can be translated "source," and *hupotasso*, which can be translated not only "to submit," but also "to behave responsibly toward another" or "to align oneself with," they refused even to entertain my suggestions. Why would ministers be so insistent on holding on to teachings that obviously cause women pain, sorrow, and sometimes death? The answer, I believe, lies in sexism. "You ought to be writing about the resistance on the part of some women to embrace their Godly roles, not attacking biblical truths," raged a pastor in rural Indiana. I'd be praised by "ardent feminists from across the country" for my "lies and distortions," prophesied another parish pastor serving in Michigan.

Curiously, six women ministers I interviewed said they also believe in and teach male headship and female submission in marriage. Wives should submit graciously to the God-given authority of their husbands, these pastors told me. Domestic violence is not caused by male headship, but is due to "some wives being unwilling to submit to their husbands in all things," a pastor serving in Illinois emphatically stated. She said that men who abuse their wives have not yet "let go of their sinful nature." When I pointed out to the pastor the irony of her beliefs—a woman called by God to be the "head" of not only female but also male congregants who is teaching women to subjugate themselves to their husbands, even when these men are abusive—she said I was putting words into her mouth. She labeled my views "social radicalism" and declined an offer to be quoted by name.

Most of the other ninety-six ministers I interviewed strongly oppose the doctrines of male headship and female submission. Like me, they believe the teachings are sexist and dangerous to women. "Male headship sets the stage for domestic violence," declared Father Michael McDermott, a Catholic priest in St. Paul, Nebraska. "I don't subscribe to that in any way, shape, or form. When we talk about a man and a woman in the sacrament of matrimony, we're talking about a partnership, people working together. One partner is just as much the expression of God's creation as the other." Rev. Julie Mall called the doctrine of male headship dangerous and discriminatory. "The teaching promotes domination and inequality rather than mutuality and partnership that the Christian Scriptures also teach," she insisted. "Scripture espouses both viewpoints just like it supports both slavery and freedom. Knowing that there's support for either domination or equality, people need to choose which view they want to give authority to, knowing that it informs how they behave. It's time we say sexism and other forms of discrimination are wrong, just like slavery is wrong." Dr. Roger Lovette, a Southern Baptist minister who pastors the Baptist Church of the Covenant in Birmingham, Alabama, says teaching anything less than equality between men and women violates the spirit of Jesus. "I don't think there's a pecking order among people of faith, with God on top, then husbands, wives, children, the dog, etc.," Lovette asserted. "We simply don't find this kind of order in the spirit of Jesus." Pastor Lovette expressed added concern about male headship and female submission in marriage. "The problem with these two doctrines is that they give license for troubled men to misuse the teachings to force their will on their wives," he concluded. "Headship and submission are manipulative tools that are very dangerous."

Clergy as Perpetrators

We're often the last ones to confide in others about our own situations. And yet, there is something we desperately need to talk about: the fact that some ministers are themselves abusers.

—REV. CLARENCE G. ROBINSON, PASTOR OF ST. MARK AFRICAN METHODIST EPISCOPAL CHURCH, MILWAUKEE, WISCONSIN

Recently, I received a phone call from a ministerial colleague who serves as the senior pastor of a thriving parish. A friend whom he has known for twenty years had just been arrested for assault and battery after beating and raping his own wife. This was not the first time the man had violated his intimate partner, my colleague told me. But it was the first time the wife had pressed charges or told anyone else about her husband's abuse. Near the end of the conversation, my colleague disclosed one further detail: the accused man was his associate pastor.

Discussing male clergy who abuse and batter their wives is taboo. It is a topic that rarely garners a whisper, even among the closest ministerial colleagues. In fact, some of the clergy I interviewed, upon learning I would be addressing this particular theme, warned me to rethink this decision. "The subject is too hot," cautioned a pastoral colleague serving a parish in Hawaii. "You'll end up making male ministers angry, uncomfortable, and may even get sued. Leave well enough alone." But isn't that a major part of the problem? I asked the colleague. For far too long ministers have been afraid to speak up or even hint about male clergy who perpetrate domestic violence. In fact, there are male ministers from all branches of service—administration, chaplaincy, counseling, education, missions, parish, and social services work—who abuse their wives. And we will never be able to become true advocates for domestic violence victims, or be able to hold perpetrators accountable for their destruction, until we acknowledge and seek help for our own problems.

"We clergy must first look at our own marriages before we can even think about helping others," insists Rev. Dan Smith. "We must stop denying the fact that, unfortunately, we have some clergy out there who are themselves abusers." Rev. Clarence G. Robinson also pointed out the importance of mutual honesty among clergy. "We're often the last ones to confide in others about our own situations," he asserted. "And yet, there is something we desperately need to talk about: the fact that some ministers are themselves abusers."

An adult corrections worker in Milwaukee with more than twenty years of experience dealing with perpetrators of various types of violence urges that clergypeople get help for their own past wounds. "Many ministers, mostly males, have not addressed their own issues, whether they are batterers, presently or formerly, or they've been raised in an abusive situation," observes Rev. Janice Brazil-Cummings, an African Methodist Episcopal deacon who serves as the Regional Director for the State of Wisconsin Department of Corrections, Division of Community Corrections. "How are we going to minister to others," she asked, "if we don't first deal with ministering to ourselves?"

One other issue must be noted. Seven of the male ministers I interviewed admitted, unsolicited, that they had emotionally, physically, or verbally abused their wives at least once during their marriage. Six of these men showed remorse over their behavior, and they seemed to be disclosing the abuse out of guilt and shame. But the other minister, who pastors a large church in the Midwest, appeared to disclose out of arrogance. "Sure, I've had to 'correct' my wife from time to time," he boasted. He justified the abuse by calling it his "Christian duty as head of my household." None of these men have ever attended a batterers' intervention program to help them address their abusive behavior. "I've apologized over and over again to my wife for hitting her and calling her degrading names, asked forgiveness from the Lord, and have tried to forget about all the hurt I've caused," confessed one of the ministers, who has served in hospital chaplaincy for twenty-five years. When I asked the chaplain if he'd ever repeated the abuse he used to perpetrate against his wife, he replied, "Unfortunately, I have, and on many occasions."

What Every Clergy Member Needs to Know about Domestic Violence

I think what many victims are looking for in ministers is for us to not only talk about domestic violence as a sin, but also for us to be willing to try and do something about it.
—REV. DR. RODNEY E. WILMOTH, PASTOR OF THE HENNEPIN AVENUE UNITED METHODIST CHURCH, MINNEAPOLIS, MINNESOTA

Taped to the front door of the chaplain residents' office at the medical center where I serve is a brochure detailing various aspects and outcomes of domestic violence. In the center section of the document, prominently displayed in bold lettering, are the words, *"You deserve to be safe."* During the writing of this book, I presented a didactic on domestic violence at the request of the chaplains. Shortly thereafter, I gave each resident a packet of material on the subject, including brochures and the phone numbers of counselors, hotlines, legal aid, and shelters located on Oahu and the Neighbor Islands. The chaplains themselves decided to affix a copy of the brochure to the front of their office door. In the first week following this simple action, five female employees of the hospital sought my assistance to help them deal with episodes of abuse perpetrated by a husband or boyfriend. The number of victims seeking help from our department has since steadily increased. In the majority of cases, the women said they were moved to seek consultation by seeing the brochure on the chaplain residents' door.

As ministers, we need to know that the emotional and spiritual support we offer victims is crucial to their overall well-being. Most victims aren't looking for us to provide miracle cures. Instead, what they have told me they need from ministers are indications that we believe their stories and that we care enough about them to obtain the necessary training in order to deal with domestic violence in an appropriate and effective manner. This does not demand that we earn a Ph.D. in psychology or mean we have to take on the impossible task of finding answers for all the complexities that domestic violence engenders. It does, however, require ministers to demonstrate acts of compassion and sensitivity: putting up brochures or fliers condemning abuse and violence on the doors of our offices, on bulletin boards in the narthex of our churches, and in the Sunday morning church bulletins; frequently including concerns about victims in our pastoral prayers; stating definitively, and frequently, from our pulpits and in classrooms that domestic violence is a sin; attending workshops and reading articles and books about the subject on a regular basis; and making resources available to victims and their children. "I think what many victims are looking for in ministers is for us to not only talk about domestic violence as a sin," contends the Rev. Dr. Rodney E. Wilmoth, "but also for us to be willing to try and do something about it."

The need for clergy and other pastoral ministers to seek appropriate domestic violence education is enormous. I shudder as I look back on the number of ministers who have told me they themselves counsel both victims and perpetrators (often together!), without ever having gone through a single training session, taken one course, or read one article, book, or pamphlet on domestic violence. How do these women and men of faith deal with the many elaborate psychological and spiritual qualities this issue presents? Unfortunately, there is a strong tendency on the part of ministers, especially those of us with little or no training in this subject, to offer highly simplistic and spiritualized solutions to very complicated problems. Thus, women being abused by their husbands or boyfriends are told by clergypeople to pray harder for a miracle; to turn the other cheek; to submit totally to these men; to present themselves as a living sacrifice; and to remember that God will not give them any more than they can bear. Due to a lack of proper training, many ministers totally fail to recognize that domestic violence, while certainly having a faith and spiritual component, is largely an issue born out of psychosocial dynamics. Are most clergy members actually qualified to deal with this problem alone?

I was once asked to speak on domestic violence by a pastor serving a very active congregation in Minnesota. About twenty lay volunteers from the church, all women, had identified this as the most critical issue facing the world as we embark upon a new century, the pastor told me. At one point during the three-hour session, several women began disclosing the episodes of abuse perpetrated by their own husbands, all of whom were also members of the church. Due to the sensitive nature of the subject being discussed, the group agreed not to repeat what was shared in the workshop to anyone outside of the room. All the group members recognized that confidentiality was crucial to the safety of the women sharing. About fifteen minutes into this deepening discussion, one of the victims talked about living seventeen years with a man who would beat her one moment and "be on his hands and knees the next, begging my forgiveness." That man happened to be one of the ordained deacons in the church. The pastor, who was seated next to me, seemed uncomfortable with the entire discussion. "I can't believe any Christian man would do such a horrible thing," the minister said in an outraged tone. "But, even if everything happened as you've said, you need to forgive your husband. After all, he said he was sorry." I met with the pastor alone after the session. The intent was to help him understand the complicated nature of abuse. But he accused me of not being guided by God's Holy Spirit because I had "encouraged the women to badmouth their husbands" and to "spread lies." He knew most of the husbands very well, the pastor told me. None of them seemed like a perpetrator to him.

As we have seen earlier, it is essential for clergypeople not only to believe stories of abuse that victims share, but also to recognize that there are in fact victims within our own parishes. "I want my brothers and sisters in ministry to keep their antennas out and start believing that there are women and children worshiping among us who are going through utter hell," pleaded Dr. Roger Lovette. "[D]omestic violence is in every church, because churches are made of people. I don't mean that Christians are worse than anybody else. We just reflect the culture." Rev. Nelda Rhoades Clarke cautioned clergy to watch their verbal cues. She noted that even though most ministers are compassionate, our words sometimes betray us. "Even comments like, 'Oh my gosh, I can't believe that!' which may simply indicate our feelings of shock, can still send the message to a victim that suggests she's not being believed," Clarke said. "So we must become more sensitive in our word choice." Father Dan Smith encourages clergy to believe victims—even if we've known their perpetrators for years. "One of the things that clergy have to do, which is sometimes very difficult, is to believe a victim's story," Smith insisted. "When a woman comes into my office and tells me she's being abused by her husband I automatically believe her, even if I've known her husband for years."

Clergy and other pastoral workers must be prepared to work collaboratively with professionals from other disciplines. Far too often, I have observed that clergypeople act as lone agents, attempting to have the answers to every whim and woe of life. This is impossible, even for men and women called by God! Clergy must remember that while an individual's spiritual well-being is vital, so is the well-being of their body and mind. All three parts must be equally nurtured if we are truly to function as whole and healthy creatures.

I am very fortunate to serve as chaplain in an institution that strongly promotes the equal value of our bodies, minds, and spirits. Often, I will receive a referral to a domestic violence situation from one of our nurses, physicians, psychologists, or social workers. These professionals recognize the important role faith and spirituality play in the lives of many victims. I recall a situation in which a female patient disclosed to a nurse that she was reluctant to have her husband come visit, because the husband always made her "feel worthless." The nurse called a social worker to further assess the woman's needs. During that meeting the patient told the social worker that her husband often derided her for "being overweight, unattractive, and stupid." The wife said she used to confront her husband about his verbal putdowns, but then he began to physically abuse her. He told his wife that "the Bible teaches wives to submit graciously to the authority of their husbands." Hearing this, the social worker referred the patient to me. I explained to the woman that no one deserved to be either physically abused or called the degrading names that her husband had called her. His actions clearly violated the way the Christian Scriptures instruct husbands to treat their wives, I said.

Eventually, the patient gave me permission to meet with the minister from her church, who had not been previously told about the abuse. Having received training in domestic violence response, the pastor was very helpful. He met with the patient and, like me, assured her that she in no way deserved her husband's abuse. After receiving permission from the wife, the minister then met separately with her husband. He encouraged the man to seek spiritual counseling from him, and batterers treatment from a group I had recommended. After the wife was released from the medical center, she joined a support group for abused and battered women sponsored by a local battered women's shelter.

"We must have an open line of communication with attorneys, advocacy groups, psychologists, and others in the community," asserts Rev. Robert S. Owens, Jr., "so that we will know where to refer victims and perpetrators." Rev. Dr. Anne Marie Hunter also stresses the need for clergypeople to build relationships with other service providers in their community. "The unique role of clergy is that we can deal with faith issues," she said. "Victims often have questions about forgiveness, marriage covenant, the interpretation of certain scriptural passages, etc. And they look to us to help them with their spiritual concerns. So clergy need to know how to respond to these faith issues, and then how to refer victims to community service providers, who also have their own unique roles in these situations." Hunter concluded that, ideally, ministers would have already spent time with service providers in their community building relationships, so that they will be prepared when crises occur.

It is important for clergypeople and those from other disciplines to recognize that no one group has all the solutions to the complex problems associated with domestic violence. By working together collaboratively, however, we can provide victims with the emotional, physical, and spiritual care they deserve. Not only can we hold perpetrators accountable for their sins, but we can also offer them the treatment and spiritual counseling they need in order to stop hurting women, children, and themselves.

Conclusion

Most ministers—females and males, conservatives, moderates, and liberals alike, from all ethnic and racial backgrounds—have done a very poor job of caring for victims of domestic violence and in dealing with those individuals who perpetrate this sin. We continue to deny the prevalence of the problem, especially within our own faith groups and among couples worshiping in our churches. We fail to recognize the connection between some of the doctrine we espouse, and the abuse and subjugation of females. And, while readily acknowledging the fear and helplessness this issue engenders, we refuse to seek the necessary training to help us care effectively for victims and confront perpetrators. We even fail to talk about or acknowledge the fact that some of our own male colleagues are themselves abusers.

Sexism and other forms of bigotry also plague us. Having grown up in a culture that perpetuates the ill-treatment of females, both in and out of Christendom, many male ministers have a difficult time fathoming the true size of the problem, sometimes suggesting that women exaggerate or even make up claims of being abused by their husbands and boyfriends. Further, at times we blame females for their own victimization. On the other hand, some female ministers also shirk their pastoral responsibilities. They say that since most domestic violence is caused by males toward females, then it should be up to men alone to fix the problem.

Domestic violence won't disappear on its own. Survivors probably won't stop blaming and punishing themselves for their own victimization, and on their own regain all the esteem that was stolen from them by abuse. Perpetrators probably won't start taking responsibility for all the damage they've caused their intimate partners and children, and at their own initiative seek batterers treatment and spiritual counseling. Both groups desperately need our support. But, in order for ministers to be effective care givers, we must first seek help for our own problems with abuse and violence, and then we must immerse ourselves in the vast amount of resources on domestic violence that are available to us.

Questions for Discussion

1. Discuss how the stories in the first section of the chapter made you feel. Which stories affected you most and why?

2. Discuss the five factors that prevent more clergypeople from becoming involved in domestic violence issues. Which of these factors do you resonate with personally and why?

3. If both a victim and perpetrator were members of your congregation, how would you address a situation of domestic violence?

4. How much domestic violence training have you yourself had? What factors have prevented you from seeking more training?

5. Do you think there are ministers who themselves perpetrate domestic violence? Have you ever known a ministerial colleague who was emotionally, physically, psychologically, sexually, or verbally abusive to his wife (or to her husband)? If you approached the individual on this matter, what did you do and say? If you chose not to talk to the person, discuss your reasons for not doing so.

6. How do you feel about collaborating with community service providers to address the issue of domestic violence? What advantages and disadvantages do you foresee?

7. What do you think every clergy member needs to know about domestic violence? Discuss why these issues are important. In what areas do you yourself need more training and why?

Notes

Introduction
1. American Medical Association, "Facts about Family Violence." Available online from <http://www.ama-assn.org/ad-com/releases/1996/fvfact.htm>.

Chapter I
1. Al Miles, "Men act like beasts; and leave women, children terrified," *The Honolulu Advertiser,* February 11, 1995, A11.
2. Nancy Nason-Clark, *The Battered Wife* (Louisville: Westminster John Knox Press, 1997), 153.
3. Old Testament scholar Phyllis Trible translates and interprets this text very differently. See Trible, "Eve and Adam: Genesis 2–3 Reread," in *Womanspirit Rising,* ed. Carol P. Christ and Judith Plaskow (New York: Harper and Row Publishers, 1979), 74-81.
4. Charles Ess, "Reading Adam and Eve: Re-Visions of the Myth of Woman's Subordination to Man," in *Violence against Women And Children,* ed. Carol J. Adams and Marie M. Fortune (New York: Continuum, 1995), 100.
5. Mary Stewart Van Leeuwen, "Promise Keepers Proof-Text Poker," *Sojourners,* January/February 1998, 16-17.
6. Carolyn Holderread Heggen, "Religious Beliefs and Abuse," in *Women, Abuse, and the Bible,* ed. Catherine Clark Kroeger and James R. Beck (Grand Rapids, Mich.: Baker Books, 1996), 18.
7. Patricia Riddle Gaddis, *Battered but Not Broken* (Valley Forge, Penn.: Judson Press, 1996), xiii.
8. Heggen, "Religious Beliefs and Abuse," 20.
9. See Gaddis, *Battered but Not Broken,* 44.
10. Terrence E. Fretheim, "The Book of Genesis," in *The New Interpreter's Bible,* Vol. 1, (Nashville: Abingdon, 1994), 345.
11. Ibid., 352.

12. Ibid., 353.
13. Ibid.
14. Ibid., 361.
15. David M. Scholer, "The Evangelical Debate over Biblical 'Headship,'" in *Women, Abuse, and the Bible*, ed. Catherine Clark Kroeger and James R. Beck (Grand Rapids, Mich.: Baker Books, 1996), 29.
16. Catherine Clark Kroeger, "God's Purposes in the Midst of Human Sin," in *Women, Abuse, and the Bible*, 207.
17. Scholer, "The Evangelical Debate over Biblical 'Headship,'" 43.
18. Ibid., 46.
19. Ibid., 49.
20. Ibid., 50.
21. Catherine Clark Kroeger, "Let's Look Again at the Biblical Concept of Submission," in *Violence against Women and Children*, ed. Carol J. Adams and Marie M. Fortune (New York: Continuum, 1995), 136.
22. Ibid., 139.
23. Van Leeuwen, "Promise Keepers Proof-Text Poker," 16.
24. Ibid., 17.
25. Catherine Clark Kroeger, "The Biblical Option of Divorce" (unpublished), 4.
26. Craig S. Keener . . . *And Marries Another: Divorce and Remarriage in the Teaching of the New Testament* (Peabody, Mass.: Hendrickson Publishers, 1991), 31.
27. Ibid., 55.
28. James Earl Massey, "The Marriage Catechism in First Corinthians" (unpublished), 29.
29. Ibid., 28.
30. Kroeger, "The Biblical Option of Divorce," 4.

The author extends a warm *mahalo* to Catherine Clark Kroeger, Ph.D., and Rev. Dr. James Earl Massey for their willingness to be interviewed for this chapter.

Chapter 2

1. A portion of this story is told in Al Miles, "When Faith Is Used to Justify Abuse," *The American Journal of Nursing,* May 1999, 33-34.
2. Ibid., 32.
3. Ibid., 34-35.
4. Julie A. Owens, "Evil—the Heart of Violence?" *Healing Ministry,* January/February 1995, 24.
5. Neil Jacobson and John Gottman, *When Men Batter Women* (New York: Simon and Schuster, 1998), 36-37.
6. Al Miles, "Violence against Women," *The Clergy Journal,* August 1999, 18.
7. Al Miles, "Helping Victims of Domestic Violence," *The Christian Ministry,* March/April 1997, 33.
8. American Medical Association, "Facts about Family Violence." Available from <http://www.ama-assn.org/ad-com/releases/1996/fvfact.htm>.
9. Bureau of Justice Statistics National Crime Victimization Survey, August 1995. Available from <http://www.ojp.usdoj.gov/bjs/>.
10. See Jacobson and Gottman, *When Men Batter Women,* 53-54.
11. See Miles, "Helping Victims of Domestic Violence," 34.
12. Al Miles, "When Words Abuse," *Leadership,* Spring 1999, 98.
13. Nancy Nason-Clark, *The Battered Wife* (Louisville: Westminister John Knox Press, 1997), 155.
14. See Miles, "When Words Abuse," 99.
15. See Jacobson and Gottman, *When Men Batter Women,* 248-49.
16. Lenore E. Walker, *The Battered Woman Syndrome,* rev. ed. (New York: Springer, 2000).
17. Ibid.

The author extends a warm *mahalo* to Debbie Hauhio, Bertha Herrera, Rev. Dr. Anne Marie Hunter, Rev. Michael McDermott, Julie A. Owens, B.A., Molly Pandorf, L.C.S.W., Rev. Bob Rooney, Rev. John Tschudy, Lenore Walker, Ed.D., and Yvonne Yim, L.S.W., A.C.S.W., for their willingness to be interviewed for this chapter.

Chapter 4

1. From Anne L. Ganley, "Integrating Feminist and Social Learning Analyses of Aggression," in *Treating Men Who Batter: Theory, Practice, and Programs,* eds. P. Lynn Caesar and L. Kevin Hamberger, (New York: Springer, 1989).
2. Al Miles, "When Words Abuse," *Leadership,* Spring 1999, 98.
3. Neil Jacobson and John Gottman, *When Men Batter Women* (New York: Simon and Schuster, 1998), 36-37.
4. Ibid., 37.
5. Ibid., 38.
6. Ibid.
7. Ibid., 38-39.
8. Miles, "When Words Abuse," 100.
9. Ibid.
10. Ibid.
11. Ibid.
12. Ibid.

The author extends a warm *mahalo* to L. Kevin Hamberger, Ph.D., Nanci Kreidman, M.A., Nancy Murphy, M.A., Melody Moody, L.S.W., A.C.S.W., Lenore Walker, Ed.D., and "Edgar" for their willingness to be interviewed for this chapter.

Chapter 5

1. Curtiss Paul DeYoung, *Reconciliation* (Valley Forge, Pa.: Judson Press, 1997), 100-101.
2. Martin E. Marty, "The Ethos of Christian Forgiveness," in *Dimensions of Forgiveness,* ed. Everett L. Worthington, Jr. (Philadelphia: Templeton Foundation Press, 1998), 9.
3. Ibid., 11.
4. Ibid., 20.
5. Frederick W. Keene, "Structures of Forgiveness in the New Testament" in *Violence against Women and Children,* ed. Carol J. Adams and Marie M. Fortune (New York: Continuum, 1995), 121.

6. Ibid., 122.
7. Ibid.
8. Ibid.
9. Ibid., 123.
10. Ibid.
11. Ibid.
12. Ibid., 124.
13. Ibid., 125.
14. Ibid., 126.
15. Marie M. Fortune, "Forgiveness: The Last Step," in *Violence against Women and Children,* eds. Carol J. Adams and Marie M. Fortune (New York: Continuum, 1995), 204.
16. Ibid., 202.

The author extends a warm *mahalo* to Rev. Fritz Fritschel, Rev. Joan Ishibashi, Everett L. Worthington, Jr., Ph.D., Rev. Dr. Laura Delaplain, Mimi Lind, M.S.W., L.C.S.W., Rev. Nelda Rhoades Clarke, Rev. Dr. Anne Marie Hunter, and "Mary" and "Cynthia" for their willingness to be interviewed for this chapter.

Chapter 6
1. Nancy Nason-Clark, *The Battered Wife* (Louisville: Westminister John Knox Press, 1997), 67.
2. Al Miles, "When Words Abuse," *Leadership,* Spring 1999, 96-100.

The author extends a warm *mahalo* to Rev. Dr. Joe Boone Abbott, Rev. Janice Brazil-Cummings, Rev. Nelda Rhoades Clarke, Rev. Dr. Peter Fribley, Rev. Fritz Fritschel, Rev. Patrick Handlson, Rev. Dr. Anne Marie Hunter, Rev. Joan C. Ishibashi, Rev. Dr. Roger Lovette, Rev. Neal MacPherson, Rev. Julie Mall, Rev. Michael F. McDermott, Dr. James D. Moebes, Rev. Robert S. Owens, Jr., Rev. Clarence G. Robinson, Rev. Bob Rooney, Rev. Dan Smith, and Rev. Dr. Rodney E. Wilmoth for their willingness to be interviewed for this chapter.

Appendix A.
Selected Resources

Adams, Carol J., and Marie M. Fortune, eds. *Violence against Women and Children: A Christian Theological Sourcebook*. New York: Continuum, 1995.

Borg, Marcus J. *The God We Never Knew: Beyond Dogmatic Religion to a More Authentic Contemporary Faith*. San Francisco: HarperSanFrancisco, 1997.

Bussert, Joy M. K. *Battered Women: From a Theology of Suffering to an Ethic of Empowerment*. New York: Division for Mission in North America, Lutheran Church in America, 1986.

DeYoung, Curtiss Paul. *Reconciliation: Our Greatest Challenge—Our Only Hope*. Valley Forge, Pa.: Judson Press, 1997.

Dobash, Emerson R., and Russell Dobash. *Violence against Wives*. New York: The Free Press, 1979.

Dutton, Donald G. *The Abusive Personality: Violence and Control in Intimate Relationships*. New York: Guilford Press, 1998.

Fortune, Marie M. *Keeping the Faith: Questions and Answers for the Abused Woman*. San Francisco: HarperSanFrancisco, 1987.

Fretheim, Terence E. *The New Interpreter's Bible*. Vol. 1: The Book of Genesis. Nashville: Abingdon Press, 1994.

Gaddis, Patricia Riddle. *Battered but Not Broken: Help for Abused Wives and Their Church Families.* Valley Forge, Pa.: Judson Press, 1996.

Jacobson, Neil, and John Gottman. *When Men Batter Women: New Insights into Ending Abusive Relationships.* New York: Simon and Schuster, 1998.

Keener, Craig S. *. . . And Marries Another: Divorce and Remarriage in the Teaching of the New Testament.* Peabody, Ma.: Hendrickson, 1991.

Kroeger, Catherine Clark, and James R. Beck, eds. *Healing the Hurting: Giving Hope and Help to Abused Women.* Grand Rapids, Mich.: Baker Books, 1998.

Kroeger, Catherine Clark, and James R. Beck, eds. *Women, Abuse, and the Bible: How Scripture Can Be Used to Hurt or Heal.* Grand Rapids, Mich.: Baker Books, 1996.

Kroeger, Catherine Clark, et al., eds. *Study Bible for Women: The New Testament.* Grand Rapids, Mich.: Baker Books, 1995.

McCullough, Michael E., Steven J. Sandage, and Everett L. Worthington, Jr., eds. *To Forgive Is Human: How to Put Your Past in the Past.* Downers Grove, Ill.: InterVarsity Press, 1997.

McDill, S.R., and Linda McDill. *Dangerous Marriage: Breaking the Cycle of Domestic Violence.* Grand Rapids, Mich.: Fleming H. Revell, 1991.

Miedzian, Myriam. *Boys Will Be Boys: Breaking the Link Between Masculinity and Violence.* New York: Anchor Books, 1991.

Miller, Mary Susan. *No Visible Wounds: Identifying Nonphysical Abuse of Women by Their Men.* New York: Fawcett Columbine, 1995.

Nason-Clark, Nancy. *The Battered Wife: How Christians Confront Family Violence.* Louisville: Westminster John Knox Press, 1997.

Plaskow, Judith, and Carol P. Christ, eds. *Weaving the Visions: New Patterns in Feminist Spirituality.* New York: HarperCollins Publishers, 1989.

Reilly, Patricia Lynn. *A God Who Looks Like Me: Discovering a Woman-Affirming Spirituality.* New York: Ballantine Books, 1995.

Walker, Lenore E. *The Battered Woman.* New York: Harper and Row, 1979.

Walker, Lenore E. *The Battered Woman Syndrome.* (Rev. ed.) New York: Springer, 2000.

Wink, Walter. *Engaging the Powers: Discernment and Resistance in a World of Domination.* Minneapolis: Fortress Press, 1992.

Worthington, Everett L., ed. *Dimensions of Forgiveness: Psychological Research and Theological Perspectives.* Philadelphia: Templeton Foundation Press, 1998.

Appendix B.
State Coalitions

National Coalition against Domestic Violence
National Office
P.O. Box 18749
Denver, CO 80218-0749
Phone: 303-839-1852   Fax: 303-831-9251
Website: www.ncadv.org

Alabama Coalition against Domestic Violence
Carol Gundlach
P.O. Box 4762
Montgomery, AL 36101
Phone: 334-832-4842   Fax: 334-832-4803

Alaska Network on Domestic Violence and Sexual Assault
Lauree Hugonin
130 Seward St., Room 209
Juneau, AK 99801
Phone: 907-586-3650   Fax: 907-463-4493

Arizona Coalition against Domestic Violence
Michele Hallett
100 West Camelback, Suite 109
Phoenix, AZ 85013
Phone: 602-279-2900   Fax: 602-279-2980
Toll Free number: 800-782-6400

Arkansas Coalition against Domestic Violence
Sharon Sigmon
#1 Sheriff's Lane, Suite C
North Little Rock, AR 72114
Phone: 501-812-0571   Fax:501-812-0578
Toll Free number: 800-269-4668

California Alliance against Domestic Violence
Susan Brazilli
926 J Street, Suite 1000
Sacramento, CA 95814
Phone: 916-444-7163   Fax: 916-444-7165
Toll Free number: 800-524-4765

Statewide California Coalition for Battered Women
Linda Berger
6308 Woodman Ave., #117
Van Nuys, CA 91401
Phone: 818-787-0072   Fax: 818-787-0073

Colorado Coalition against Domestic Violence
P.O. Box 18902
Denver, CO 80218
Phone: 303-831-9632   Fax: 303-832-7067

Connecticut Coalition against Domestic Violence
Linda J. Cimino
106 Pitkin Street
East Hartford, CT 06108
Phone: 860-282-7899   Fax: 860-282-7892
Toll Free number: 800-281-1481

Delaware Coalition against Domestic Violence
Carol Post
P.O. Box 847
Wilmington, DE 19899
Phone: 302-658-2958   Fax: 302-658-5049

DC Coalition against Domestic Violence
Sandra A. Majors
513 U Street NW
Washington, DC 20001
Phone: 202-387-5630   Fax: 202-387-5684

Florida Coalition against Domestic Violence
Lynn Rosenthal
308 E. Park Avenue
Tallahassee, FL 32301
Phone: 850-425-2749   Fax: 850-425-3091
Toll Free number: 800-500-1119

Georgia Coalition on Family Violence
Alisa Porter, Exec. Dir.
1827 Powers Ferry Rd. Bldg 3
Atlanta, GA 30339
Phone: 770-984-0085   Fax: 770-984-0068

Hawaii State Coalition against Domestic Violence
Carol C. Lee
98-939 Moanalua Road
Aiea, HI 96701
Phone: 808-486-5072   Fax: 808-486-5169

Idaho Coalition against Sexual and Domestic Violence
Sue Fellen
815 Park Blvd., Suite 140
Boise, ID 83712
Phone: 208-384-0419   Fax: 208-331-0687
Toll Free number: 888-293-6118

Illinois Coalition against Domestic Violence
801 S. 11th St.
Springfield, IL 62703
Phone: 217-789-2830   Fax: 217-789-1939

Indiana Coalition against Domestic Violence
Laura Berry
2511 E. 46th Street, Suite N-3
Indianapolis, IN 46205
Phone: 317-543-3908   Fax: 317-377-7050
Toll Free number: 800-332-7385

Iowa Coalition against Domestic Violence
Laurie Schipper
2603 Bell Ave., #100
Des Moines, IA 50321
Phone: 515-244-8028   Fax: 515-244-7417
Toll Free number: 800-942-0333

Kansas Coalition against Sexual & Domestic Violence
Sandy Barnett
820 SE Quincy, #600
Topeka, KS 66612
Phone: 785-232-9786   Fax: 785-232-9937

Kentucky Domestic Violence Association
Sherry Allen Currens
P.O. Box 356
Frankfort, KY 40602
Phone: 502-695-2444   Fax: 502-695-2488

Louisiana Coalition against Domestic Violence
Merni Carter
P.O. Box 77308
Baton Rouge, LA 70879
Phone: 225-752-1296   Fax: 225-751-8927

Maine Coalition to End Domestic Violence
Tracy Cooley
170 Park St.
Bangor, ME 04401
Phone: 207-941-1194   Fax: 207-941-2327

Maryland Network against Domestic Violence
Michaele Cohen
6911 Laurel Bowie Rd., #309
Bowie, MD 20715
Phone: 301-352-4574   Fax: 301-809-0422
Toll Free number: 800-634-3577

Jane Doe, Inc./Massachusetts Coalition
Marianne Winters
14 Beacon St., #507
Boston, MA 02108
Phone: 617-248-0922   Fax: 617-248-0902

Michigan Coalition against Domestic and Sexual Violence
Mary Keefe
3893 Okemos Rd., #B-2
Okemos, MI 48864
Phone: 517-347-7000   Fax: 517-347-1377

Minnesota Coalition for Battered Women
Marcelle Diedrich
450 N. Syndicate, Suite 122
St. Paul, MN 55104
Phone: 651-646-6177   Fax: 651-646-1527
Toll Free number: 800-289-6177

Mississippi Coalition against Domestic Violence
Michelle Baker Carroll
P.O. Box 4703
Jackson, MS 39296
Phone: 601-981-9196   Fax: 601-981-2501

Missouri Coalition against Domestic Violence
Colleen Coble
415 E. McCarry
Jefferson City, MO 65101
Phone: 573-634-4161   Fax: 573-636-3728

Montana Coalition against Domestic & Sexual Violence
Kathy Sewell
P.O. Box 633
Helena, MT 59624
Phone: 406-443-7794   Fax: 406-443-7818
Toll Free number: 888-404-7794

Nebraska Domestic Violence and Sexual Assault Coalition
Sarah O'Shea
825 M Street, Suite 404
Lincoln, NE 68508
Phone: 402-476-6256   Fax: 402-476-6806
Toll Free number: 800-876-6238

Nevada Network against Domestic Violence
Sue Meuschke
100 West Grove St. Suite 315
Reno, NV 98509
Phone: 775-828-1115   Fax: 775-828-9911
Toll Free number: 800-230-1955

New Hampshire Coalition against Domestic and Sexual Violence
Grace Mattern
P.O. Box 353
Concord, NH 03302
Phone: 603-224-8893   Fax: 603-228-6096
Toll Free number: 800-852-3388

New Jersey Coalition for Battered Women
Barbara M. Price
2620 Whitehorse Hamilton Sq. Rd.
Trenton, NJ 08690
Phone: 609-584-8107   Fax: 609-584-9750
Toll Free number: 800-572-7233

New Mexico Coalition against Domestic Violence
Mary Ann Copas
P.O. Box 25266
Albuquerque, NM 87125
Phone: 505-246-9240   Fax: 505-246-9434
Toll Free number: 800-773-3645

New York State Coalition against Domestic Violence
Sherry Frohman
Women's Building
79 Central Avenue
Albany, NY 12206
Phone: 518-432-4864   Fax: 518-463-3155
Toll Free number: 800-942-6906

North Carolina Coalition against Domestic Violence
Karen Luciano
301 West Main St., Suite 350
Durham, NC 27701
Phone: 919-956-9124   Fax: 919-682-1449
Toll Free number: 888-232-9124

North Dakota Council on Abused Women's Services
Bonnie Palecek
418 E. Rosser, #320
Bismarck, ND 58501
Phone: 701-255-6240   Fax: 701-255-1904
Toll Free number: 888-255-6240

Action Ohio Coalition for Battered Women
Phyllis Carlson-Riehm
P.O. Box 15673
Columbus, OH 43215
Phone: 614-221-1255   Fax: 614-221-6357
Toll Free number: 888-622-9315

Ohio Domestic Violence Network
Nancy Neylon
4041 N. High Street, #400
Columbus, OH 43214
Phone: 614-784-0023   Fax: 614-784-0033
Toll Free number: 800-934-9840

Oklahoma Coalition on Domestic Violence & Sexual Assault
Marcia Smith
2525 Northwest Expressway, Suite 208
Oklahoma City, OK 73112
Phone: 405-848-1815   Fax: 405-848-3469

Oregon Coalition against Domestic Sexual Violence
Margaret Brown
659 Cottage Street, NE
Salem, OR 97301
Phone: 503-365-9644   Fax: 503-566-7870

Pennsylvania Coalition against Domestic Violence
Susan Kelly Dreiss
6400 Flank Drive, #1300
Harrisburg, PA 17112
Phone: 717-545-6400   Fax: 717-545-9456
Toll Free number: 800-932-4632

Commission Para Los Asuntos de la Mujer
Box 11382, Fernandez Juancus Station
Santurce, PR 00910
Phone: 787-722-2907   Fax: 787-723-3611

Rhode Island Coalition against Domestic Violence
Deborah DeBare
422 Post Road, Suite 202
Warwick, RI 02888
Phone: 401-467-9940   Fax: 401-467-9943
Toll Free number: 800-494-8100

South Carolina Coalition against Domestic Violence and Sexual Assault
Vicki Bourus
P.O. Box 7776   Columbia, SC 29202
Phone: 803-256-2900   Fax: 803-256-1030
Toll Free number: 800-260-9293

South Dakota Coalition against Domestic Violence and Sexual Assault
Verlaine Gullickson
P.O. Box 141
Pierre, SD 57501
Phone: 605-945-0869   Fax: 605-945-0870
Toll Free number: 800-572-9196

Tennessee Task Force against Domestic Violence
Kathy England Walsh
P.O. Box 120972   Nashville, TN 37212
Phone: 615-386-9406   Fax: 615-383-2967
Toll Free number: 800-356-6767

Texas Council on Family Violence
Pam Willhoite
P.O. Box 161810
Austin, TX 78716
Phone: 512-794-1133   Fax: 512-794-1199
Toll Free number: 800-787-3224

Utah Domestic Violence Advisory Council
Diane Stuart
120 N. 200 West, #319
Salt Lake City, UT 84103
Phone: 801-538-9886   Fax: 801-538-4016

Vermont Network against Domestic Violence and Sexual Assault
P.O. Box 405
Montpelier, VT 05601
Phone: 802-223-1302   Fax: 802-223-6943

Women's Coalition of St. Croix
Mary Mingus/Cloma S.
P.O. Box 2734 Christiansted
St. Croix, VI 822
Phone: 340-773-9272   Fax: 340-773-9062

Virginians against Domestic Violence, Inc.
Kristi Van Audenhove
2850 Sandy Bay Road, Suite 101
Williamsburg, VA 23185
Phone: 757-221-0990   Fax: 757-229-1553
Toll Free number: 800-838-8238

Washington State Coalition against Domestic Violence
Mary Pontarolo
8645 Martin Way, NE, Suite 103
Olympia, WA 98516
Phone: 360-407-0756   Fax: 360-407-0761
Toll Free number: 800-886-2880

West Virginia Coalition against Domestic Violence
Sue Julian/Diane Reese
4710 Chimney Drive
Charleston, WV 25302
Phone: 304-965-3552   Fax: 304-965-3572

Wisconsin Coalition against Domestic Violence
Mary Lauby
307 S. Paterson St., Suite 1
Madison, WI 53703
Phone: 608-255-0539   Fax: 608-255-3560

Wyoming Coalition against Domestic Violence and Sexual Assault
Rosemary Bratten
P.O. Box 236, 710 Garfield, #242
Laramie, WY 82073
Phone: 307-755-5481   Fax: 307-755-5482
Toll Free number: 800-990-3877